SPANNER

A Dales Lad to Bomber Command and Back

Len Watson

SPANNER

A Dales Lad to Bomber Command and Back

Len Watson

His Story – By Len & Gill Watson

© Gillian Horner, 2011

Published by Horner Enterprises (Leeds)

A CIP catalogue record for this book is available from the British Library.

ISBN 978-0-9570849-0-2

Prepared and printed by:
York Publishing Services Ltd
64 Hallfield Road
Layerthorpe
York YO31 7ZQ

Tel: 01904 431213

Website: www.yps-publishing.co.uk

I hope you like this book.
It has been written with a happy heart;
and a sense of humour and a few tears

In the Beginning.............

A little boy was born in Bedlam.

Spanner was born in Bedlam on 20th March 1922 which was certainly appropriate. He was often reminded of his place of birth by his family when he became the source of subsequent bedlam in his life, which he was, frequently. He was named Leonard Newby Watson and was the first born son of Newby and Jenny Watson.

Bedlam is actually a small village on a hill, near Ripley on the Harrogate to Pateley Bridge road at the entrance to Nidderdale, which is one of the most beautiful of the Yorkshire dales.

I am Gill, Spanners daughter. His family called him 'our Leonard' but as it is a long long time before I can call him Dad I shall call him Leonard to avoid confusion.

Leonard's father was a farm labourer and the family lived in tied cottages that 'came with the job' which meant they moved every time his job changed. Unfortunately Newby's job came to an end about a year after Leonard was born and as a result the family moved to Ninevah near the glorious spectacle of Fountains Abbey for a very short period of time before again moving to Brighouse. It was just fifteen months after Leonard's birth that his younger brother Herbert came into the world on 11th June 1923.

Herbert was an 'eight month baby' and in those days it was always thought that they were delicate and prone to illness. That was the way at the time and it led to many a child being cosseted. Herbert was a bit spoilt and pampered, but Leonard wasn't fazed by it and they got on well as children.

Leonard remembers *"when 'e were born mi mother insisted that our 'erbert sleep with 'er as 'e were to be nurtured and that meant I 'ad to sleep with mi father. Mi father let me fall out of bed and there were such a bang on t'floor and there were 'ell to pay from mi mother. Mi mother used to tell this story and it still mecks mi laugh.*

Our 'erbert never did show any unusual proneness to illness, any more than me, but 'e soon learnt 'ow to milk being spoilt. If anything went wrong it were allus my fault and I remember one day he threw a gripe (pitch fork) at me in t'orchard, so I off after 'im and 'e ran into t'house at back door shouting to mi mother that our Leonard's going to 'it me – so I got a scut (clout) It didn't really bother me though, our 'erbert were alright"

So that was the rather unremarkable start of 'our Leonard'. I am not sure how the falling out of bed affected him but he was certainly to lead a very eventful life thereafter.

He hung on fervently to his Yorkshire accent all his life as if to let it go would be sacrilege and a gross betrayal of his roots.

CERTIFIED COPY of an ENTRY OF BIRTH.

Pursuant to the Births and Deaths Registration Acts, 1836 to 1874.

Registration District *Tadley Burg*

1922 Birth in the Sub-District of *Dacre Banks* in the County of *York*

No.	When and Where Born.	Name, if any.	Sex.	Name and Surname of Father.	Name and Maiden Surname of Mother.	Rank or Profession of Father.	Signature, Description and Residence of Informant.	When Registered.	Signature of Registrar.
62	Twentieth March 1922 Search Bank Clint RD	Kenneth Roy	Boy	Newby Watson	Jane Watson Watson formerly Peacock	Farm Labourer	Newby Watson Father Search Bank Clint	Twentyfifth April 1922	George E Wilkinson, Registrar,

I, *George E Wilkinson* Registrar of Births and Deaths for the Sub-district of *Dacre Banks* in the County of *York* do hereby certify that this is a true copy of the Entry No. *62* in the Register Book of Births for the said Sub-district, and that such Register Book is now legally in

WITNESS MY HAND this *25ᵗʰ* day of *April* 19.22

George E Wilkinson Registrar of Births

Birth certificate

Halcyon Days of Markington

The family were on the move again and their next move was to Markington to Haddock Stone Grange farm.

Leonard remembers *"I allus thought it were a strange name to give a farm as there were no water anywhere near it and not a sign of any 'addock, and I did look"*

The farm nestled in a dip just out of Markington village. The farm no longer exists but there is a farm called Haddock Stone farm in existence today nearby. The farm was big by standards of the day. There were fifty acres of ploughing land that Newby worked on, stretching down into a small valley across to Hob Green.

The family lived with the farmer, Johnny, in the farmhouse. It was a large farmhouse and had a big kitchen and Leonard used to ride his father's bike round and round it on a wet day.

"I remember there were a big boiler in t' wash 'ouse outside the back door"

Leonard and Herbert used to go off to the school in Markington dressed in their short trousers and little caps. It would have been about a mile walk to school from there; *"it were five field lengths and a bit o' main road. There were only one car in t' village in them days, down at the bottom shop, and the main means of transport were 'orse, 'orse and cart or shank's pony"*

Leonard used to doff his cap whenever he met someone on his way to school it as it made him feel very grown up. He says *"It got back to mi mother and she were reet proud of me. I were a polite little lad"*

They used to climb trees a lot, run around the fields, paddle in streams *"and put dams in them of course"* he says. They also used to play cricket and were very proud that their Dad was in Markington cricket team. *"mi father were pretty good, 'e usually opened the batting and 'e allus won the annual batting average every year"*

The two boys used to run home after school as they loved to run to where their father was working ostensibly to help him and ride the horses back in, at walking pace of course.

"the 'orses were so wide that our legs used to stick straight out at sides and we 'ad to 'old on very 'ard"

Ploughing was done by horse and plough; there were very few tractors around then. Their father did all the ploughing and would be raking it in night and morning. In later years they got some trap horses as well – Lucy and Dolly.

"mi father used to tek milk every Sunday morning to Harvey's through Markington. Sometimes 'e used Lucy and sometimes Dolly. There were a bit of an 'ill and Lucy used to gallop up it. One morning mi father were tekkin the milk and using Dolly. Dolly shied at cars and she used to tek off if she were tethered in a trap, as she did on this morning. Mi father tried to 'old 'er up and 'e pulled back on t'reins. Reins broke and Dolly were off. Each day when Dolly took the milk they would stop at t' post office to get a paper. Well when Dolly took off mi father didn't know what 'e were going to do, but Dolly stopped dead outside t' post office as usual! 'orses aren't that daft.

The farm had seven horses altogether. Farmer were t' biggest one – he could pull t' plough hisself, and they allus used to plough up the 'eadlands in them days, which they don't do now, right up to t'edges. Mi father used to tek 'Farmer' round t'edges. Another were called 'Captain' and he were a bit lighter than t'others. He were a farm 'orse and if 'e were in t'stall mi brother would get up side of 'im and climb in t'manger and 'e could stroke 'im while 'e were eating – 'e took well to mi brother. If 'e were laid out in t'field loose mi brother could go and sit on 'is back – 'e were that sort of 'orse. Another were 'Smiler' and 'e were an excellent trace 'orse. The trace 'orse is up at front, there'd be two 'orses – cart 'orse in t'shafts and trace 'orse for extra pull at front"

Farmers usually had guns which they kept mainly to go rabbiting to supplement their income and to kill rats that were prolific on farms.

"Mi father 'ad a little two two rifle, it were a smooth bore and you could use either cartridges or bullets in it. After threshing day all t' corn went into a grainery up some steps and men used to carry bags of corn from t' threshing machine along a passage and up into t'grainery. After this mi father used to go out with 'is gun and I used to go with 'im. There were two sizes of cartridge you could get – little'uns and big 'uns – mi father used little 'uns for this. 'e used to go in to t'grainery with this gun – a garden gun we called it. He 'ad the gun in one 'and a torch in t'other and 'e used to shoot rats running up t'wall and he even 'ad time to reload with one 'and shoot again as they ran up t'wall. He were a good shot mi father"

Leonard used to use this gun and go round the land looking for the rabbits which were numerous. He used to crawl very slowly to see how close he could manage to get to the rabbits and then he would shoot them. He also used to sit outside rabbit holes and wait for them to come out, which seems a bit mercenary but the end result was a dead rabbit whichever way you looked at it. More rabbit was eaten than chicken in those days.

Once Leonard saw a stoat which had caught a rabbit so he shot the stoat and took the rabbit off it. His father did a lot of rabbit snaring and he would take Leonard with him sometimes. It meant going out on a morning and then again at night and Len used to help carry the rabbits back. His father would set the snares again and there would be rabbits in them again next morning. Newby used to go up the dale rabbiting with ferrets and most of the rabbits went to market as the farmers used to make their rent with them. They used to have plenty of rabbit pie and they also kept hens so eggs were in abundance. This was long before the myxomatosis blighted the rabbit populace.

The farmer eventually married his cousin and Newby lost his job in the process so they had yet another move.

Leonard, Newby, Jenny and Herbert – the first family picture

Leonard's favourite picture of his Dad – 2nd left at bottom

Leonard emulates his daddy

Newby plays host to a cart load of girl guides

Sheep shearing in the 20's

It all looks so peaceful – tranquillity between the wars

Newby in Home Guard uniform with a gun in those same tranquil fields

School Days

At Markington School Leonard managed to get caned occasionally for climbing up on the school roof. Whenever balls got stuck on the roof of the school Len, with typical bravado, volunteered himself to get them, without much argument from the less intrepid. This meant climbing the building and negotiating several drops and rises peculiar to a many-roofed building, and then sliding down to the back of the relevant chimneys to get the balls; hence the caning. Health and Safety and Human Rights have put paid to such antics – no more climbing roofs or caning, which is a shame. Leonard would be the first to say it did us no harm.

Markington School – Leonard is kneeling bottom left

He doesn't remember much about his later schooling at Summerbridge other than he learnt to play the trumpet and was in the school band. He was also in the school cricket team and usually opened the batting along with Eric Gill the captain, the same as his father did for Markington.

Another Markington school picture – Leonard is on the middle row far right and Herbert is on the bottom row third from right.

Leonard says "I used to get out of school early for singing with Joyce (third from left on top row)"

Leonard and Herbert a little older and with Boys Brigade sash, belt and hat

Newby and Jenny all dressed up

13

A Family Between Wars

So now we have a family of Mum, Dad and two children growing up in Yorkshire in the years between the two world wars. Effects of the 1st world war were still in evidence however they did not adversely affect the Watsons as much as those living in towns and cities.

In 1930 there were over 2 million people unemployed, which is a phenomenal figure bearing in mind that the population in England was 39 million. In 2010 England had a population of over 51 million and had suffered an upsurge in unemployment as a result of yet another recession. It rather puts the vastness of the unemployment in 1939 in perspective. The unemployment continued through the 'in between' years and, at the outbreak of the 2nd World War, was still at 1.25 million.

These were depressing times but also times of change and progress. An appreciation of little things was more apparent. If you wanted light you had to use candles or oil lamps. If you wanted heating you had to lay a fire and light it and clear out the ashes afterwards. If you wanted a bath you had to fill a tin bath with hot water which took a lot of time. If you wanted clean clothes you had to wash them by hand or in a wash tub with a wooden dolly (like a small stool but with a long handle that was pushed into the wash tub and turned in the clothes to agitate them). If you wanted water you had to carry it from a source. If you wanted to go to the toilet you had to go to an outside toilet shed and use newspaper for toilet paper. If you wanted an apple pie you had to bake it. Life was much more of toil.

Standards of living were rising through the advent of new aspects to ways of life. A major change was electricity. However by 1933 only 1 in 3 homes had an electricity supply but this changed over the successive years.

Hartwith

The family were on the move again, this time to Hartwith when Leonard was about ten years old. They moved into a lovely cottage – Cow Close Cottage at the entrance to the lane to Cow Close Farm where Newby's new job was. The cottage was about half a mile from the main Harrogate/Pateley Bridge road and there was a regular bus service each way. The boys went to school in Summerbridge about 3 miles away towards Pateley and a bus used to pick them up at the end of Stripe Lane each morning.

Leonard has very fond memories of Cow Close Cottage.

He remembers *"it 'ad a stream to cross to get to t' front garden and there were some stepping stones. I could run across those stepping stones in t' dark and never get mi feet wet. I thought I were very clever!*

I do remember that mi mother worked very hard. She were allus washing, cleaning and cooking. She made some wonderful pies, cakes and scones. She also made a lot of jam and apple chutney. We used t'keep all the picked apples on newspapers in t' attic ready for cooking. She looked after us well. If we 'ad a birthday party, and we 'ad one or two friends there, I remember mi father allus used to say 'come on, reach to, but tek one mind' – I'll never forget that phrase"

The cottage lent itself to some creative use. Focal point was a big black range in the living room which was common in a lot of homes. This provided heat, hot water, an oven and a swing-arm trivet on which the kettle could be heated on over the fire. Next to the range was a small room which was the coal house.

Leonard had the bright idea of changing this coal house into a makeshift bathroom. Up until this time bathing was limited to a tin bath in front of the fire and filled with water heated by the fire in the range boiler. This obviously incurred a privacy problem. Well Len's bright idea was to put one of the new white enamel baths in this coal house room. There was a drainage problem though and to get round it he ran a waste pipe from the plug through the wall and directly into the stream.

"Nearest we kem to 'aving a bathroom" says Leonard.

He hadn't finished at that though. He had managed to commandeer a small room down the side of the cottage outside as a workshop.

"I spent a lot of time in mi workshop fixing things and constructing things, usually including mechanical objects that did not allus work as they should. There were some unusual contraptions to come off mi production line. Mi next idea were to get more light into mi workshop, so I devised a way to get electricity in. I constructed a wheel in t' stream and attached that to a bicycle dynamo and I got mi electricity!"

The farmer at Cow Close was called Willy Lumley and Leonard remembers he tended to look down on the Watson children as their father was a farm labourer so they never spent much time at his house. He did however have a son, George, and he and Leonard became firm friends.

"George once got scarlet fever and 'e allus blamed me for giving it to 'im and I never 'ad it! Dr. Petch were my doctor and I never 'ad to go to the fever 'ospital but George 'ad to. My Uncle Frank and Aunt Lizzie ran the fever 'ospital up on t'moors. Mi mother played 'ell when she found out George were blamin' me and then Willy's father 'ad to tell 'im off, but it didn't matter to me"

IF IT

'IF IT' became the 'our Leonards' next adventure into construction, this time on a bigger scale.

Willy had an old Jowett Bradford which was so old that it only had one door and a square box body. He used to take it to Harrogate each week to sell rabbits and butter.

He eventually took the body off his van and used it for a hen house and he sold the engine leaving just the wheels and chassis.

Leonard relates *"I 'ad an old motorbike with an engine and I 'ad an idea to use it to drive a circular saw, but instead of t' circular saw I decided we'd put together a vehicle. Me an' George put an old Governors cart body on the back of the Jowett chassis and a seat on the back which were on pegs. It were a bit Heath Robinson as it really took two to drive it. I 'ad the steering wheel and brake which were on t' prop shaft, and George 'ad the gears and accelerator, but you 'ad to reach over the tank to change the gears. I were the only one who could drive it on mi own and I used to go round the farm and to t' buildings and down the lane. We used to push it up t' lane, we couldn't afford petrol, it was 1s 6d per gallon. We screwed the carburettor top off by 'and, then we pushed it and let brake off and it allus started first time. We allus thought it weren't going to start so we christened the car IF IT – short for IF IT STARTS. When it started and ran a second or two we 'ad paraffin by tap in t' motorbike tank – the tap were like a pencil that ran through the top of the tank. When it started we took it outa gear and let it run for a bit on paraffin and then when we set off each of us would put 'is foot outside and we eased it off, touched the gear and it would tick over and we'd be off!*

Girl Guides used to come to camp in summer months and they used to walkover to Cow Close farm to get milk. *"we offered to give 'em a lift back on IF IT. What we did was chug up t'hill and we'd turn it around and then it would go faster, but the back seat used to jump out of t'pegs and these lasses used to fall off t'back – oh we did laugh. By gum we 'ad lots of laughs in them summers"*

IF IT did get a lot of use. They used to drive across the fields to the woods to fetch firewood home. *"but we daren't stop it, so when we got to the gates the one handling the gears would jump off in front of it while it were moving, open the gates and then close them and run like billio and get back on again"*

When there was snow on the ground Leonard upped his developing ingenuity and made a snow plough. He would take IF IT up to the top of a hill, turn round, put the plough on the back and then clear the snow so that the sheep could get to eat the grass. Willy Lumley was very pleased with this but it didn't really seem to change in his attitude towards the boys.

IF IT and left to right – Herbert, Newby, George and Mrs Horsfield (a friend)

While all this was going on and Len was busy growing up and building strange and wonderful contraptions in his little shed things were changing radically in the big bad world. Like a small amoebic mass gathering momentum political unrest was dominant in many countries.

Leonard says *"I weren't on these pictures as I were tekkin 'em!"*

"Mrs Horsfield's husband were the 'ead of the Fire Brigade at Wakefield and when I got a motorbike I became the despatch rider for the Brigade. I were there when the first bomb were dropped on Wakefield, it landed on the football field"

No casualties there then.

IF IT and Left to right – George, Herbert, Mrs Horsfield and Newby

Employment

He left Summerbridge School at fourteen having achieved the dizzy heights of 'above average'. When he left he got a job working for his cousin, Stan Richmond in Pateley Bridge, doing painting and decorating for the princely sum of 5/- (five shillings) per week. He used to ride his bicycle the seven miles to work. Stan's workshop was situated at the top of Pateley Bridge High Street next to the old brewery. The brewery had the distinction of being a major Pateley landmark – a tall chimney, which unfortunately has since been demolished in keeping with the times. When Leonard started work he then became known as Len.

Len says *"when I were working for Stan the little sweetshop at the top of t' High Street in Pateley Bridge had two bikes for sale, one were a BSA three speed and t' other were a 28" wheel bone shaker. So I bought 'em both for 25 shillings and I took 'em 'ome one at a time cycling to Hartwith. Later on John, who worked for Matt Hastings, told me that Ronnie Dale had an Hercules hub-braked tandem for sale, so I got in touch with 'im and he swapped 'is tandem for one of mi bikes! Me and George used to go all over on that tandem. We used to go to Arrigut* (Harrogate) *to t' pictures on t' bike. If we went on t' bus it only kem back on the bottom road so we 'ad to get off at Birstwith and walk 'ome via Ross bridge in t'valley bottom and up to t' top road and to Hartwith"*.

This tiny little sweep shop at the top of Pateley High Street, known as the oldest sweetshop in England, is still there today.

Len refers to the 'top road' which was the route taken by the No. 23 bus from Harrogate to Pateley Bridge and used to run sparsely. The other route – route 24 on the bottom road, used to run (and still does to this day) hourly. The route 24 road runs along one side of a very wide valley from Birstwith and the route 23 road, and from Stripe Lane end runs along the other side of the valley a bit higher up until both roads converge at Summerbridge. Both roads can be seen from each other from these points to Summerbridge. To get from Birstwith on the bottom road across to the other side of the dale to the top road Len used to ride his bike, or walk, often in the dark along a lane which crossed the river Nidd at Ross bridge and then the railway line, which was in existence in those days. Walking in the dark in the country can be quite spooky but it was a way of life they were used to.

It may seem that much is devoted to describing the top and bottom roads and the buses to Pateley but to Dales folk it was their link to the outside world and their way of getting about the dale. The times of the buses dictated many lives.

"We also used to go on our bikes to Kettlesing on a Sunday night to a dance and we 'ad t' be back 'ome by 10 o'clock. We used to finish up at t' bus shelter at Dacre Top playing mouth organs. That's where I learnt to play the mouth organ and I got pretty good at it. And that bus shelter is still there! "

Another place they used to go was down to Matt Hastings farm primarily because he and his assistant John used to tinker with vehicles. This was like a magnet to Len. *"One day Matt told John that they were selling new bikes at auctions so John started thinking and 'e asked Matt if 'e would buy 'im one if they were still selling 'em. So Matt agreed but John 'ad to pay 'im back for it of course. He brought it up t' show me – so I showed 'im mine. 'is didn't 'ave three speeds like mine and 'e said 'e liked mine better than 'is new un, so 'e said I'll swap you. Well I thought I could sell 'is new 'un a bit easier than my old 'un so I agreed"*

Len eventually left Stan Richmond's as he wanted to work in joinery and managed to get a job at Arthur Addyman's in Harrogate and this meant he was riding his bicycle eight miles in the other direction. He was 16 years old by this time and on a slightly higher wage.

He was working on the benches, not going out to jobs, and he was at work when war broke out. Arthur decided there and then to pack in, which he did for the duration of the war, so at five o'clock Len cycled home and everybody finished. Arthur Addyman's business is actually still going today.

Meanwhile, in the Rest of the World

Whilst this is Len's story the evolvement of Spanner came about as a result of what was going on in the rest of the world. So it is perhaps prudent to have a rudimentary look at what was happening in other countries between the two world wars.

After the First World War there was promising growth in the form of democracy which saw many countries including Austria, Russia and Germany embracing a republic state in place of the overthrown autocratic regimes. There were in fact seven newly created states in Europe that adopted the republican form of government. It was however not destined to last. Some kind of dictatorship took over many democratic countries in the period between the two wars. Germany and Italy became Fascist states and Russia became a Communist state all labouring under the heading of totalitarianism. France and Britain remained as the only Democratic states.

Democracy means – freedom of speech and of course the press and freedom from arrest for political opinions. Political parties could be newly formed and election of parties was encouraged.

Totalitarianism means – No freedom of speech or freedom of publications. No rights to form political parties. Only one governing body of a dictatorial nature existed imposing total rule. Religion, work, leisure and private life was ruled by the state. The individual had no rights and only existed to serve the state.

Russia, Italy and Germany were strong totalitarianism states. Thus we have a pot simmering away of states with different ruling bodies getting more disenchanted with other states not embracing their ideals.

There were also other underlying insurgencies simmering in individual countries.

Russia – The rise of totalitarianism in Russia has its basis well back in time. Two and a half centuries of Mongol rule did nothing to discourage it. Russia was socially and economically backward and had a history of autocratic rule. There was an urge therefore to modernise but without the foundation of the expertise to carry it out. To add to the confusion there was also an inherent resistance to modernisation. The borders of Russia were insecure and open to invasion and geographically and culturally they were never a fully European country. This in turn created huge insecurity amongst the populace and thus there was an authoritarian determination to extol control as being the only answer. Under Stalin, Russia became one of the most brutal and repressive totalitarian states. On November 30th 1939 Russia invaded Finland with a force of over 600,000 men backed by air and naval power. This was in support of the Finnish Peoples Government which was sponsored by the Soviet Union. Finland asked the League of Nations to intervene, to which they eventually agreed, but the Soviet Union opposed its involvement and thus was expelled from the organisation.

Italy – became Fascist – the rise was as a result of discontent with government before the first world war and failure in both foreign and domestic affairs. The Italians wanted a strong government and Mussolini was an opportunist waiting in the wings. Mussolini proclaimed 'everything within the state, nothing against the state, nothing outside the state' and people should believe, obey and fight. People should subject themselves to the absolute authority of the state. Mussolini built up his own power within the government.

At the end of the First World War Italy was very dissatisfied with the territorial settlement that had resulted from the peace conference in Paris. They had expected big gains and the Treaty of London promised them many colonies, including some in Germany that they did not ultimately get. As Italy was poor in natural resources and lacked fertile land the loss of colonies they had expected to have fuelled the resentment, and there was huge unemployment with many emigrating. Mussolini wanted more territories to redress the balance. He invaded Abyssinia in 1935. The formation of the Rome-Berlin Axis followed in 1936. He then began infiltrating Albania which he eventually overran in April 1939. He declared war on Britain and France in 1940.

Germany – suffered a huge depression after the 1st world war. It was widely believed that this was as a result of fallout from the 1st world war.

Nazism – encompassed extreme nationalism, unification of all German speaking people into a single empire, superiority of the Aryan race, hatred of all Jews whom it blamed for all Germany's problems, and embraced an absolute belief in its destiny to be the supreme master race. Any opposition to the party was immediately squashed and terror and violence reigned to rule. This was totalitarian Fascist ideology at its strongest and its principal was Adolph Hitler with his National Socialist German Worker's Party (1920 – 1945). Hitler created jobs by expelling Jews, insisted women should stay at home to concentrate on family and young men were sent to labour camps to work. Persecution of Jews continued and trade unions were abolished. Hitler then renounced the Treaty of Versailles and began armament production in earnest in the Rhineland.

On September 1st 1939 Germany invaded Poland. Britain and France immediately issued an ultimatum to Germany demanding its withdrawal from Poland. This was ignored and Britain and France declared war on Germany. Australia and New Zealand also declared war on Germany.

Churchill's immortal words announcing to the British people that we were at war were broadcast on 4th April 1939.

World War II had begun.

Millions were destined to die.

Munich Accord

Neville Chamberlain was not a politician of the ilk of a war leader. He was in power at this time and tried to appease Hitler's demands. He procured a document signed by him and Adolph Hitler dated September 30th 1938 which he believed would ensure 'Peace for our Time' which he promised the British people. Never was Hitler's duplicity more apparent than now as he continued his build up to war in flagrant ignorance of this pact he had signed.

This is the infamous Munich Accord signed by both leaders.

"We, the German Fuhrer and Chancellor and the British Prime Minister, have had a further meeting today and are agreed in recognising that the question of Anglo-German relations is of the first importance for the two countries and for Europe. We regard the agreement signed last night and the Anglo-German Naval Agreement as symbolic of the desire of our two peoples never to go to war with one another again. We are resolved that the method of consultation shall be the method adopted to deal with any other questions that may concern our two countries, and we are determined to continue our efforts to remove possible sources of difference and thus contribute to assure the peace of Europe"

This was signed by A. Hitler and Neville Chamberlain and dated September 30th 1938. Luckily for England Winston Churchill was waiting in the wings.

Phoney War

Britain had begun preparation for the prospect of war and in January 1937 £1,500 million was allocated for defence over the following five years. Defence rather than offence was being addressed. Fear of gas attacks also preoccupied Britain's defence programme and some 150,000 gas masks were being produced every week from 1937. The British army still only numbered 897,000 against Germany's 4.5 million. It was expected that at the onset of war Britain would suffer some sustained bombing. At the end of the First World War huge casualties were inflicted from aerial bombardment and the strength of the Luftwaffe fuelled the speculation that at the start of the Second World War a massive bombardment would ensue.

Householders had to black out their homes and there was a huge run on blackout material. ARP (Air Raid Precautions) wardens patrolled the streets and shouted at households where a sliver of light showed at their windows. All street lamps were unlit and vehicles had to screen their headlights and buses and trams had to screen any interior lights. Torches were initially banned but this rule was eventually relaxed if the torch was covered with two layers of tissue paper. Torch batteries became impossible to buy and people refrained from venturing out in the dark for fear of getting lost. Emergency ambulance services were set up and other services such as repair and demolition along with first aid posts and of course rescue.

The expected aerial bombardment did not transpire immediately and some of the people who had been evacuated began drifting back home. This period became known as the phoney war.

The operation to 'get the children away' began in September 1939 and became known as 'Operation Pied Piper'. Posters were produced saying 'Caring for Evacuees is a National Service'. Those agreeing to take evacuees were given small payment and it was illegal for anyone to refuse an evacuee if they had room. The country was divided into 'danger zones' such as major cities and industrial areas, whereas rural and coastal areas were regarded as safe and therefore 'reception areas'

Throughout the war Pathe News reels ensured that the people had constant reassurance that we were winning. Radio broadcasts were a huge contribution to the spirit of the people and music and entertainment played a big part in the feel good factor that it was imperative to support.

Huts for Evacuees

Now that war had broken out and young Len was unemployed, he went to the labour exchange in Millfield Street in Pateley. They sent him to Bewerley Park where wooden huts were being erected to house evacuees from the Leeds area.

The firm that was running the job was Beaumont and Wilson based on Glebe Road off Cold Bath Road in Harrogate. Len says *"foreman were t' bosses son, Billy Wilson"*

It is quite amazing how we can remember finite details from long ago yet struggle to remember what happened yesterday. Thankfully Len manages to remember very many details of his life over the next few years.

"One little story were when I were there I were putting shutters up and windows all round and tee 'inges and whistling away to misself. I were trying to loosen a screw by just tapping it a few times with an 'ammer, and someone said "what's your screwdriver for?" I said "to take the bloody things out with" and giggled, I didn't realise it were the boss that 'ad asked me! – luckily nothing more were said but I could 'ave got sacked for that.

The huts came on wagons every morning from Arrigut (Harrogate), *so they picked me up at the bottom of Stripe Lane on their way to Pateley, so it were good for me. When the work in Pateley finished I were invited to start working in the workshops in Arrigut* (Harrogate), *so I were back to cycling there.*

It were about this time that mi mother and father took in an evacuee. A little girl called June came to live with us. She were a quiet little thing and we all automatically felt very protective of 'er. I remember making some toys for her to play with"

June's Story

I was five years old and I had started school earlier that year. Suddenly I kept hearing the word 'war' being mentioned everywhere and I wondered – what was 'war'?

I was going to school as usual one morning and I can remember being told to stand in line in two's, and we had favourite toys with us. Then we were ushered off and we walked for two miles from Leeds Parish Church to the station. I thought we must be going on a school outing, which looked like it could be fun but nobody told us where we were going.

It was very exciting when we got to the railway station and seeing lots of Mams and Dads waiting there with carrier bags and cases and parcels. I was very bewildered and wondered what was going on, though the excitement overcame this. I asked Mam if I could have a penny for a bar of chocolate from the machine, I remember that part so well, but after that it is a bit hazy as I do not remember anything of the train journey. I remember being in a school hall with lots of noise and people talking loudly. There was lots of hustle and bustle and we were given a drink of cocoa and a biscuit but I wondered – where was my Mam? Gradually the noise became less as grown-ups and children were slowly leaving and eventually, when we were down to about five left we were taken off in a car with our bags and cases. One or two children were dropped off along the way and after a nice ride we turned down a lane that led to a farm, but I didn't know it led to a farm then. The car stopped and I was helped out with my belongings. It is from this moment on that I cannot recall missing my mother, perhaps I did, but I do not remember.

I got out of the car at the side of a lovely stone cottage and there was a stream that had to be crossed by stepping stones which was brilliant fun for my five year old mind. There was a gate at the other side; it was a big gate, more like a door, with a sneck to open it. We went through the gate into a garden which was full of flowers, and seeing all the colours it was like a rainbow had fallen down, it was just like magic. The cottage door was wide open but no-one was there so I was told to wait inside and that someone would be coming soon. I decided to look in my carrier bag and saw a new toothbrush and toothpaste. Then I spied a small stool and the sink and if I stood on the stool I could reach the sink and tap. I stood on the stool to clean my teeth and I had the brush in my hand and a mouthful of toothpaste when the lady of the house, Mrs Watson, came back and found me.

I soon settled in as it was a lovely place and Mr and Mrs Watson were very nice kind people. They had two sons Leonard and Herbert who were older than me and they treated me very well. Leonard made me some toys and I remember a money box made out of wood, it had a swivel piece on it. Leonard also taught me how to knit!

We had some lovely food as Mrs Watson cooked a lot. There was a big range with hooks and there was often a cauldron hanging on it with sheep's head broth or soup or stew cooking. We ate pies and cakes and teacakes as well. I used to play in the orchard and there was a swing on an apple tree. I also used to go up to the farm and play with a girl called Freda.

I would often go up the road with Mrs Watson to feed the hens and at Easter I was lucky enough to get a pink egg laid especially for me. They were very clever hens; I only had to ask them. I was even taken to the pictures (cinema) in Harrogate for a birthday treat.

One day Mr Watson said they had been having trouble with a fox as it was after the chickens. Some days after this he caught the fox and brought it into the cottage and laid it on the rug to show me, it was so colourful and I remember shades of orange, I wasn't frightened at all. At bed time he would bring in a jug of milk straight from milking the cows and we often had home-made cake to go with it.

Every Wednesday a van would come round with groceries and things, obviously it was limited because of rationing but to my little mind it was more magic. I spent my sweet coupon on a stick of Maynard's liquorice, this was round with a flat piece at the end, and I put it on top of a cupboard and each day I would have a little bite.

I had to go to school of course and a taxi or bus used to take me to school. When it was a taxi it was brilliant because the taxi had some little fold down seats in the back as well as the normal seat and I always sat on one of these, I felt like a queen. I remember waiting with Freda and the milk churns at the top of the lane and the old man who lived in a cottage close by used to bring out hot scones and other treats for us. I found out then that the school I had first arrived in was the school I would be attending, it was Summerbridge School.

I think I was a very lucky girl as my husband Jim was also an evacuee and he did not have such a good time of it. His school closed completely and his mother did not see him off. He cannot remember going to the station but he travelled from Leeds to Tuxford and was placed, along with his sister, with people who did not want them. These people were of such a mind that they actually took both Jim and his sister back to Leeds and dumped them on the doorstep. This was a very unpleasant experience for two children aged 6 years and 8 years respectively. Yes I was a very lucky little girl.

I had been at Cow Close Cottage for about two years and one day they said I was going to live at another house. I did not know why and I wondered if I had done something wrong. For many years I believed it was because Mr and Mrs Watson were retiring. I was transferred to Mr and Mrs Dean's house in Pateley Bridge. Mrs Watson came to see me each week for a few weeks and then she stopped suddenly. I didn't know it at the time but it was because they had to move as Mr Watson's job had ended as the farmer's son was taking his job.

Mrs Dean had two sons Norman and Wilfred. Norman became a local hero. One day I went to the cinema in Pateley and when I got home I was told about what Norman had done. Some children were swimming in the river and a girl got into difficulty. Norman and his friend swam to help and Norman managed to get the girl but his friend was drowned. Norman was awarded a lifesaving certificate but it was very sad about his friend.

The Deans were lovely people and I was very happy there. I was there until the end of the war and I grew to love Pateley Bridge visiting very many times in latter years. When the war finished a taxi came and a few evacuees were put in it and taken back to Leeds.

My father and mother lived in Quarry Hill flats in Leeds. My father worked on shifts on the railway and my mother also worked, so when I went back to the school I had the door key on a piece of string round my neck. When I got home from school I would let myself in and there would be some sweets on the table for me. I used to eat the sweets and sit and cry. One day my Dad came home and caught me crying and asked me what the matter was. I told him I was very sad for having left the Dean's so my Dad decided to go and see them. Mrs Dean asked to adopt me and my Dad said yes but when he put it to my Mam she said no. I did however go back to stay with the Deans for another couple of years, which I was very happy about.

One day I got a letter from my mother and in it she wrote to say she was having a baby and would I like to go back and help her look after it. I was 12 or 13 years old at this time. I thought a new baby could be quite exciting and I told Mrs Dean that I thought I would go back. I did go back but I visited the Deans many times which meant an hour's bus journey from Leeds to Harrogate and another hour's bus journey from Harrogate to Pateley. Many years later the Deans left Pateley Bridge and went to live in Middlesbrough, but not before they told me that Leonard was living in Pateley Bridge which was a lovely surprise. I got in touch with him and we have kept in touch ever since.

Pateley holds such happy memories for me that when Jim and I married we went to Pateley to the Deans for two days for our honeymoon. It was Pateley feast (fair) weekend when Nidderdale show was on. We are celebrating our diamond wedding anniversary in 2012. Time rolls on so quickly.

The evacuee years are so vivid to me that I wrote a poem about them. In later years I submitted it to the Poetry Guild and it was published in "Evacuee 1939-1945" in A CELEBRATION OF POETS. I was later invited to be inducted as an International Poet of Merit and Honoured Member of the International Poets Society for 1998 at the eighth Convention and Symposium in Washington DC. I was unfortunately unable to attend but am proud of the recognition.

This is my poem;

> *In two's we stood in the railway station.*
> *A country village was our destination.*
> *War was starting, loved ones parting,*
> *Goodbyes were said to Mums and Dads.*
> *And as we waited in the station*
> *Clutching toys, bags and cases, gas mask*
> *Boxes, and of course our names on tags.*
> *'Why, what for?' was on our faces.*
> *Bewildered, puzzled but excited off we*
> *Went to our new homes.*
> *Time went by, a day, a week, the years.*
> *Some were homesick and unhappy, and*
> *Quite often lots of tears.*
> *But some, like me, were very happy,*
> *Loved and cared for we were lucky.*
> *Then came the last 'all clear'*
> *War had ended, voices raised in cheer.*
> *Now a word, a smile, a face, a place,*
> *An old refrain, reminds me of the years*
> *Gone by, and I am taken back again*
> *Once more down memory lane.*

The Ministry of Health had calculated that aerial bombardment would result in 600,000 people being killed and 1,200,000 injured. This proved to be a gross over-estimation but it did serve to fuel the need for evacuation of children. Some 650,000 children were evacuated as a result.

It was a pleasure to tell June's story, particularly as it is just one story amongst thousands that evacuees can relate of their experiences of such heart wrenching displacement at such young ages. Not everyone had the fortunate experience that June had, as her husband has confirmed.

June mentions Quarry Hill flats where her parents were living. These flats became a huge landmark in Leeds over the years and people in that period will doubtless remember the circular area fronting onto the bus station. The flats were modelled on Karl Marx Hof flats in Vienna and were the largest housing development in the country at the time. They had solid fuel ranges, electric lighting, a comprehensive refuse disposal system inbuilt and of course communal facilities. They were started in the 30's and some were ready for occupation by 1938. They were built of steel framing with concrete cladding which proved to be disastrous and eventually the flats were pulled down in 1978.

Back in Harrogate

While Len was working on the benches on Glebe Road in Harrogate the boss, Mr Wilson, called him into his office.

Len says *"I thought – eyeup what 'ave I done, I 'ope I'm not going to get the sack"*

He was to get a pleasant surprise as Mr Wilson asked him if he would be prepared to work away from home and that he would double his wage if he would. Len was on 17/6d per week by now and the prospect of doubling his wages far outweighed any concerns he had about working away from home, so off he went. He was sent with another joiner's apprentice to Pinderfield's Hospital in Wakefield where huts were being erected at the top end of the asylum.

"We used to walk up some paths at the side of the asylum to work. There were often residents walking about the grounds daily and one man were regularly walking around pushing a wheelbarrow upside down. One day 'e were near to t' fence so I asked him "what are you wheeling that barrow upside down for?" and 'e touched side of 'is nose in a secretive gesture and said "I'm not daft, if I turn it t'other way up they'll put something in it"

Ah.

Len had a big time chuckle when he told this story.

Len was lodging for the princely sum of 25/- (twenty five shillings) per week. Every Saturday dinner time he would jump on his bike and cycle back to Hartwith with his washing on the back. His mother used to wash and iron his clothes for him over the weekend and he used to cycle back with them to Wakefield on Sunday afternoon. He worked at Pinderfields until the huts were finished and then he was sent to Mirfield, Huddersfield and Dewsbury.

Len says *"It were advertised in t' paper that a man in Wakefield wanted to swap a motorbike for a tandem, which sounded too good an opportunity to miss, so I got in touch with 'im and 'e said that if tandem were as good as I said it were then he'd swap me. He walked the tandem back to Wakefield and I got a 500 cc side valve Royal Enfield with a sidecar!"*

Lens next job was to work on ack ack units in Huddersfield, Dewsbury and Sheffield areas. They got lodgings in a village at Cosy Nook. Lens workmate did not drive so he rode on the back of Len on his motorbike.

"At another place on a camp there were three soldiers and a corporal sharing a bungalow and we went to live with them for a short while as we couldn't get lodgings. They 'ad very little rations other than bread and margarine, so for three days we were fed fried bread. The soldiers were supposedly guarding ack ack guns which were telegraph poles sticking out of sod heaps made to appear like gun stations. We thought they really were guns. Stores nearby were made to look like garrisons ".

Camouflage

Camouflage became an integral part of defence in all countries and very many methods were employed with great effect. This was addressed so seriously that a Corp, consisting of painters, artists and architects, was set up by the Allies specifically to address it.

In the field of battle vehicles were painted to blend in with their backgrounds and in winter snow covered areas, vehicles were painted white. In fact troops could be almost invisible when dressed all in white.

Britain on the home front used the telegraph pole camouflage in many places. The pill boxes, which were armament stores, were camouflaged and painted on the outside as shops; some were florists with flowers painted on the outside and with a trading name across the top, others were grocer's shops etc. and doubtless there were many other disguises used.

From the air everything appears as a flat canvas and it was easy to disguise even vast areas.

Old war equipment was utilised for decoy work and tanks were produced as quickly inflatable dummies. Whole military installations could be 'produced' very readily which appeared completely convincing. In fact in desert areas it was virtually impossible to gauge the size of an illusionary military installation as there was nothing in close proximity for comparison.

Germany opted for turning street areas green in efforts to appear rural. Even Leizensee Lake was enveloped as an urban landscape with lawns created and roofs built on stilts. They even went to the extreme of building decoy towns. One decoy used regularly was to light fires in unoccupied rural areas to give the impression of activity and lure bombs.

One specific camouflage Germany used was as a result of a grand gesture of Churchill's wherein he said Britain would not bomb the castles of the Rhine.

There are very many castles that sit on top of both sides of the Rhine Valley. A railway runs along the valley directly on the banks of the river. This was a vital arterial link for transport of war hardware and raw materials for the German war effort. The Rhine Valley is quite beautiful and there are steep sides with the castles only just visible in the distance on the tops from the river. Because of the steepness, and the fact that the valley becomes a gorge in places, the railway has to run into tunnels on some river bends and out the other side. At the entrance and exit of these tunnels Hitler, in his wisdom, had castle turrets erected to disguise the railway. It is not certain whether Britain ever did bomb this railway.

Much of bomber commands attention was centred around the Ruhr valley where war hardware factories were more prolific.

Joining Up

When the First World War broke out there was quite a stampede of young men wanting to join up, but the Second World War was a different story. Enthusiasm was lacking and Britain's regular army was in dire straits. In April 1939 the Military Training Act came into force which stated that all men would be liable to be called up on their 20th birthday. Strangely this act increased the number of volunteers as people realised they would be called up anyway. Volunteers usually got to choose which service they joined but it was the army that needed men and that is where most recruits were posted.

When Len joined up it was as a result of a little bit of thinking and a feeling of inevitability and all he really needed was a small push in that direction. He wanted to join the RAF and he thought he would have more chance if he volunteered.

Now that Len had a motorbike he started to go to many different places with the other joiner on the back. One day a man they were working with said to Len *"best thing you can do lad is join up"*. This made Len think more about it and the next time he was going through Leeds he went to volunteer. It was 19th July 1941. *"I told 'em I wanted to join the RAF. They asked me a lot of questions and I told 'em I were a joiner and eventually they said best thing I could do were go in for a flight mechanic on airframes – there were a lot of timber in them air frames at that time and me being a joiner made sense, so I did as they said"*

When Len told old Mr Wilson that he'd joined up he blew his top.

"Mi father were an 'ome Guard sergeant at Burnt Yates near 'artwith. Mi mother and father were not visibly upset because they were expecting

it, but I reckon they probably were upset. Our Bert joined up too. He were an 'airdresser and went into t'air force as an instrument repairer. My rank was AC 2 (Air Craftsman 2) and eventually I got to be LAC (Leading Air Craftsman) before further promotion.

I were lucky to get into the RAF because that is what most people wanted to do when they joined up. I 'ad to do quite a few tests before I were accepted. Then I were sent to do basic training in Filey. We 'ad lots of laughs in Filey. We were in civvy billets in hotels. Butlins camp 'ad been taken over by the RAF, but I were in Filey itself"

The men used to have to parade for baths in a tin shed. In the shed were two rows of pipes smattered with small holes a little like old fashioned gents toilets. They had to put their clothes in one room and all of them had to go under the shower at the same time. Then they had to get dressed and march back. *"One day me an' another lad decided we'd 'ave a better bath than that so we went to where the officers were. When no-one were looking we each popped into their bathrooms, locked t' door and 'ad a bath. When we'd finished we opened the door just a little bit to make sure nobody were in t' passage and came out. It worked out and we didn't get caught"*

A cinema car park became their parade ground and their rifles for rifle drill were kept in a hut. They carried out rifle drill with Polish rifles of which there were two sizes and the ones they used were the short ones.

"On one particular occasion there were a sergeant stood on a box bellowing at us. I 'ad cut mi thumb at 'ome on a razor blade and it must 'ave opened up as I felt something dripping into my shoe, so I glanced down. The sergeant saw me and bellowed out at me. I raised mi rifle to what we called 'trail arms' (just lifted off t'floor) and I marched straight up to 'im on 'is box and he were gettin' redder and redder. When I got up to 'is box I put mi rifle down and stood to attention as you do and I showed 'im mi thumb bleeding and dripping. 'e changed 'is tune immediately and said "now there's a lad that's been trying" He told me to put mi rifle away and go down to the M O's and get mi thumb properly dressed. The lads were all stood in rows and I went round the back of the sergeant and grinned and I waved at 'em"

"When the training finished we 'ad to scrub out 'otels ready for the next recruits to come in, but as I were waiting to go on a flight mechanics course I got off that and were given a job in the quarter masters store dishing clothes out. After that I got to be in the sports store and Dave Scrawley were in charge of the store. He were only a little fella but he were a boxer. He were due to be in a fight and the Air Force wouldn't let him fight so he said "bugger the Air Force" and 'e went. He were a grand little fella and 'e taught me a lot about boxing".

Len was eventually sent to Squires Gate in Blackpool.

Training in Blackpool

Blackpool became the RAF's largest training area with camps at Weeton and Kirkham. At the outbreak of war the site was taken over by 63 squadron flying Battles and 75 and 215 squadrons flying Wellingtons. The ministry of aircraft production built a Vickers Wellington shadow factory in 1940 and Wellingtons were built on the site until it closed down. Today the site is in use as Blackpool Airport and houses industry and shopping centres.

The men were put into civvy billets and every morning they were required to parade outside the pleasure beach. They were taken by bus to Squiresgate. They were also required to carry identity cards at all times for which spot checks were carried out. This was Len's undoing. *"I were checked once and, sods law, I 'ad forgotten my card so I were put on jankers for two to three days. I 'ad to parade up and down the pier at night. It's the only time I 'ad jankers"*

He recalls that the food wasn't too bad though it did get better as time went on. He actually developed a liking for porridge with cheese on of all things.

"We did get to go out a little bit but we were allus up early on a morning so it were limited. We 'ad no mess do's but we sometimes 'ad dinner by the pleasure beach. I also used to go to Blackpool Tower dancing to Reginald Dixon and that's where I learnt to dance mainly. I also used to go to the Lido Baths where t' dance hall went over t' baths. I once got some raffle tickets there and one came up and I gave rest of mi tickets away. They all kem up, 'ows that for a coincidence. All mi mates got 'em"

Len had been seeing a girl from Killinghall, Margaret Burns, but he did not get to see her too often as it all depended on leave. They decided to get engaged which was probably a rather rash decision, but when you were young and in a war situation all normal criteria went out of the window.

Len says *"I 'ad a dancing partner in Blackpool called Sadie. She were a lovely Irish lass but I realised she were getting a bit close to me so I thought it were only right to tell 'er that I were engaged. She lived at the north shore and I lived at south shore and she cried all the way back 'ome when I told 'er. I felt really bad"*.

Len passed out as a flight mechanic and was then transferred to Dumfries in Scotland.

Dumfries

In Dumfries Len spent his next spell of life in the RAF working on Boffers and Hansons. He also did a lot of D I's (daily inspections of aircraft)

Margaret, Len's fiancée, came up to Dumfries to see him once and he travelled home to see her, but they decided to end their engagement. Len did not feel it was right to be engaged due to the instability of being in the forces.

Len met Margaret more recently and she told him she'd never forgotten him. She had eventually married a soldier and been very happy. He wrote to her once and in error he put a blank page in. *'she said I can't 'ave been talking to her on that page!'* Margaret used to send Christmas and birthday cards until she sadly passed away.

At the beginning of the war ex-maintenance staff from the First World War were invited to come back in again and were paid £10 for this.

Len says *"A corporal that were in charge of us on the flight were one of 'em, 'is name was Corporal Rankin – I've never forgotten that"*

One day a Boffer that Len was working on came in with fault brakes and Corporal Rankin started telling him what to do.

"I told 'im that if I did as 'e said it would still 'ave faulty brakes". He said "I'm not annoyed at you but I've had lots of complaints about brakes and if you think you can put it right Watson you can get on with it. So I did it right and a test pilot took it up and he said it were ok. I kept on doing the D I's but Corporal Rankin used to come after me and pester me to finish any D I's I were doing and work on another plane that 'ad come in with faulty brakes. I were getting fed up of working on brakes.

One day he kem down to me and said "Flight Sergeant wants to see you in his office" so I thought to misself what 'ad I gone and done this time. I knocked on 'is door and he shouted me to come in. I went in and 'e looked up and said "Corporal Rankin says you are the best on the flight on hydraulic brakes so I'm going to send you to No. 3 hanger and give you someone to help you". The bloke 'e sent to help me were an LAC and 'e were useless. I thought blow this I don't want to be on brakes all the time"

Len was a bit disgruntled by this time and decided to put in for a fitters course so he filled in an application. You could not get promotion until you became a fitter, but he got an answer back saying he could not go on a fitter's course until he had been on a station for six months. It was nearly six months at this point so he waited until the time had elapsed and applied again and he was still turned down. He did not give up and he applied a third time.

After his third application he was called in front of the CO (Commanding Officer) and he looked at this third application and he said, in a posh CO voice, *"you are determined to go on a fitters course aren't you Watson"* to which Len replied *"Yes Sir – I can't 'ave any promotion until I become a fitter, I've to be LAC and then a flight engineer is as far as I can go"* His CO said *"I'm going to let you go on the strong recommendation that you come back to this station"*

Len chuckled *"I didn't go back"*

He went back to Squiresgate in Blackpool on his fitter's course and passed out over the required 80% and became an AC1 but as he was already an LAC he didn't lose his rank. It was about now that the four engine planes came out.

All Len wanted to do was fly Lancasters.

After this Len volunteered to become a flight engineer. Normally they only took sergeant fitters to train to become flight engineers but they had lost so many men that they brought the rank down to corporal/land corporal equivalent to army. There were three men going in for flight engineer.

Len says *"I remember one of 'ems name were Anthony Martin – 'e were a big Scots lad and the other were a Welsh lad. We all went together to Kirton in Lindsey near Lincoln. I were the first to go to Blackpool. What 'appened to the other two I don't know, probably didn't survive. Would be nice to know that they did"*

Life in Britain continues......

While Len was pursuing his new role in the RAF much was happening in the rest of Britain.

Rationing and supply shortages were affecting everyday living as the people knew it. In 1939 fuel was rationed and 'Motor Spirit Ration Books' were issued to taxi operators. Private motorists, who had no necessity for a car, were given a 'basic ration' to cover 1,800 miles per year, but even this was withdrawn in July 1942 for the rest of the war. Bicycles were worth their weight in gold.

As for food this was a complicated business. The government were hesitant about introducing food rationing as they were uncertain how the public would react but ultimately it had to come into force, which it did on 8th January 1940. This was initially in the form of coupons for a shopkeeper to remove from an individual's ration book, but as this caused quite a bit of work shopkeepers eventually just stamped ration books. Bacon, sugar, butter, meat, cheese, jams, syrup, treacle and tea were all rationed. Milk and eggs were 'allocated' because they were seasonally affected for availability. All these were introduced at different times and varied in allowance as the war continued. It was hard work for women to feed their families and they had to do a lot of forward planning and become quite inventive with basic supplies. Fruit and vegetables were not rationed but obviously subject to availability as with everything. Shopping meant standing in endless queues.

Flight Engineer

Len went to factories for a fortnight where they were building Lancasters. They attended school in the morning and then they went round the factory in the afternoon with an instructor advising them.

He eventually passed out as a flight engineer with a mark over 80% which was the same as another lad. They were sent, along with others, to Scampton. They both wanted Lancasters and as Len was an ex-fitter he got a choice.

It is a good job he achieved 80% as that was the pass mark that had to be achieved. Any not achieving this did not go any further.

Len says *"it's sad but I don't know whether the other lad survived or not"*

He wanted Lancasters from the very beginning because he knew that the flight engineer was also the second pilot.

They went into a big hanger into the Lancaster section, most of the engineers wanted Sunderlands.

The crew selection system was very haphazard and not at all as expected. All prospective air crew covering all trades were gathered in one room and crews generally milled around selecting themselves. It is a system that did appear to work as all crews needed to gel and get on well with each other. This presented the best case scenario for good team selection as there had been failures in crew selection in the past using a different method. Len remembers men milling around and slowly forming groups. *"There were two flight lieutenant pilots who's crew were already formed, but they'd been trained on two engines to go onto four and I'm certain they knew who to look for because their flight left"*

"Flight Lieutenant Millington kem in to choose his crew. Eventually 'e kem to me and asked me if I'd like to be 'is flight engineer. F/Lt Millington says in his book 'Was That Really Me' that I said "I'm good with tractors" and that was why I got the job!

F/Lt Millington then took me outside and introduced me to the rest of his crew"

Learning to Fly

In 1944 the crew went onto Stirlings first for training. They spent a lot of time familiarising themselves with the aircraft. The engineer wasn't 'up front' next to the skipper in a Stirling but half way down the fuselage. A Stirling was a manoeuvrable aircraft at a low altitude but it did not have the ceiling of a Lancaster. Everything ran off electric motor and they had 127 fuses and you had to know them all. The Lancaster in comparison only had 48 fuses so was a bit easier to cope with. The training period was only a fortnight and during the first week Len was required to be the second and watch another flight engineer, then in the second week he was the senior engineer training another engineer.

After this initial training they were posted to Syerston which was where Wing Commander Gibson was also posted.

Len says *"I remember that Wing Commander Gibson were a bit of a stickler and he insisted that an airman salute 'im if he should pass by. Woe betides the airman who did not comply. He did command a lot of respect though"*

Training consisted of flight after flight of practice take-offs and circuits and landings. Combat manoeuvres and cross country flights followed and they did night circuits and landings. They did cross country fighter afield, with the spitfire trying to shoot them down with canon guns, and hits were registered if the spitfire got them. There was air to sea firing and Len even had a go at the machine guns especially in the tail. This gave him a scope on what the tail gunner would have to endure when they were in battle for real.

"when you got in and turned that turret you felt as though it were falling off! It were bloomin' cold in it as well, they had electrically heated suits for rear gunners and the mid uppers"

After this he transferred onto his beloved Lancaster. Again circuits and landings and general flying continued on the Lancaster. He did local flying and cross country flights with landings at other aerodromes. He had many flights with F/Lt Millington and many test and acceptance flights.

They also did practice high level bombing around the Orkneys.

This continued through May and June. They did not do much in Stirlings and after that course they went to a squadron to start operations.

They were posted to 49 squadron.

So young and at war

Spanner is Born

L en says *"The crew I'll never forget –*

"Skipper were F/Lt Millington, he were a brilliant pilot and an excellent skipper and we felt as safe as we could be in 'is hands.

I were t' Flight Engineer and now I were where I wanted to be.

The Bomb Aimer were Scotty, 'e were an officer and he 'ad been a bank clerk before 'e joined up, he were a short, quiet chap and got on well with everyone.

The Navigator were Jimmy and he often 'ad plenty to say, and 'e were a likeable chap.

The Wireless Operator were Basil Williams and 'e 'ad been a milkman, Basil were allus the cheerful one, 'e were mi mate, we got on well.

There were two gunners – one were Blondie who 'ad lied about his age and joined up before his 18th birthday and he joined the crew fully trained a month before his 18th birthday. 'is story were a bit sad as 'e 'ad lost all 'is family in an air raid over Portsmouth and that's why 'e joined up. Blondie didn't like Americans on account of they got more interest from the girls and 'e once got 'imself into a scrap with an American outside a pub. Best bit were they both 'it out at same time and both went down together! He 'ad to live that one down afterwards!

The other gunner were Ginger on account of 'e 'ad a full 'ead of red 'air. He were quiet and reserved.

Blondie and Ginger were a bit of a double act. Once we'd gone out for a drink with t'Skipper and when we kem out Blondie and Ginger were in a field of bullocks trying to ride 'em! I got 'em out and Skipper were alright about it but it were pretty funny.

53

We kem to work as a team and each depended on the other, we were a well-oiled machine and on a few rare occasions we did get 'well oiled' and it did us good now and then!

I kem to be the one who 'ad to keep 'em in line as I were t' oldest"

Len was always a bit of a stickler and meticulously careful about his job and would not leave the aircraft on return without full checks. Vehicles transported them from the aircraft so the lads could not leave until the checks were finished. They often got a bit fed up waiting and said *'come on Spanner get a move one'*

Thus Spanner is born, that was his nickname and so he stayed throughout the war.

They were posted to Bruntisthorpe initially, without the gunners, where they were put first on the two-engine Wellington. The Wellington was later replaced by the four-engine Stirling and eventually by the Halifax and Lancaster. The Wellington was nicknamed the 'Wimpey' after the cartoon character of J. Wellington Wimpey and was a heavy aircraft with excellent manoeuvrability. All crews thought their aircraft was the best and were encouraged so to do. Little friendly arguments and banter often cropped up between crews on this subject.

The crew, along with others, were billeted in quite big huts and they had a round stove at each end.

"We used to be given stuff to do between ops. When we got up first thing I 'ad t' do was go see the skipper and report. He also 'ad me looking after his car so I had to maintain that. Because I were the Warrant Officer I got t' be in a little room at the end of an 'ut"

The saddest thing was that when Len woke each morning he couldn't help but count how many beds were empty.

It was soul destroying for them and he often wonderered how they managed to keep their spirits up.

Waiting to go on an operation affected them all in some way. Some acted the goat and others were very quiet but a lot of the lads got a bit twitchy which was understandable.

"*I often thought I were never going to come back and every one were mi last. I did get wind up a few times but once you got in your aircraft you just got on wi your job*"

After an operation they would go to put their parachutes away and then go to debriefing.

Spanner says "*We'd sit around a table with an intelligence officer and we'd tell 'im what we'd seen and if anyone 'ad shot a Geri down it would be logged. Anyway when that were finished we went to 'ave a meal, which we were all ready for as some of the flights were pretty long and many were at night. Then we went to bed. It's when we woke up that were the worst, that's when you knew who 'adn't come back*"

Spanners favourite picture

Len   Basil   Scottie   Skipper Group Captain Jimmy Ginger Blondie

Len is on the left purely because he had just jumped out of the aircraft for the picture. He was up to his usual business of checking and re-checking everything in the plane prior to take-off.

Another line up on front of the beloved Lancaster
Spanner is 2ⁿᵈ from left and some ever attentive ground staff have joined them

The Lancaster

To Spanner the Lancaster was an excellent aircraft. He developed such a proprietary feel for each Lancaster he flew in that he almost felt it was his plane. It was certainly his responsibility as he saw it.

The Lancaster was the only four engine bomber that would do one air mile per gallon of petrol. It had six tanks, three tanks each side. These consisted of outboard or wing tip tanks which held 114 gallon each, centre tanks which held 383 gallons and then the inboard tanks which held 580 gallons. It was not possible to run on the outboard tanks. With a total of 2,154 gallons it was taken that the Lancaster would fly 1,000 miles out with 1,000 miles back.

Spanner says *"I used to tek off on the inboard tanks and run for an hour, then I'd go to the centre tanks and run for two hours, then I'd pump 114 gallons from each wing tip tank into to the centre tanks and ensure level petrol in each.*

Some of the lads smoked but Skipper didn't like smoking. I didn't mind so much but I wouldn't let 'em smoke for the first hour of flight"

It was Spanners duty to keep the Skipper updated all the time on the state of the aircraft; this included any information he had as to whether any flak damage had been sustained, in fact anything that might affect the handling of the aircraft. He had to make engine adjustments, handle the fuel, constantly check all the fuses and monitor the oxygen levels. The trimming tabs could be used independently on each side to adjust if fuel was lost at one side and not the other, but this did not always work. All the crew were very vigilant when they were flying. The noise the aircraft generated was phenomenal, but Len said it is something you got used to and you were concentrating heavily on your job.

The duties of the Flight Engineer were to:

1. Monitor the engine and make adjustments as necessary throughout the flight
2. Log any and all adjustments
3. Monitor the temperature gauges
4. Monitor the oxygen levels
5. Monitor all the fuses
6. Complete a log every twenty minutes
7. Advise the Skipper of any and all changes to the condition of the aircraft
8. Transfer fuel at relevant times from outer and middle tanks
9. Fly the aircraft if required

FLIGHT ENGINEER'S PANEL, LANCASTERS I AND III

Flight deck instrument panel – A maze of gauges, knobs, buttons and switches

1. Annemeter	2. Oil pressure gauges
3. Pressure-head heater switch	4. Oil temperature gauges
5. Coolant temperature gauges	6. Fuel contents gauges
7. Inspection lamp socket	8. Fuel contents gauge switch
9. Fuel tanks selector cocks	10. Electric fuel booster pump switches
11. Fuel pressure warning lights	12. Emergency air control
13. Oil dilution button	

Contains public sector information licensed under the Open Government Licence v1.0

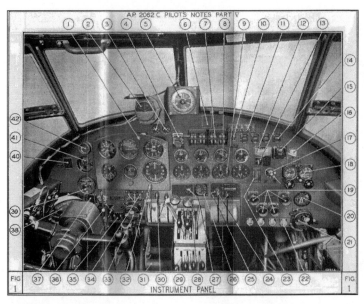

1. Instrument flying panel
2. D.F. Indicator
3. Landing light switches
4. Undercarriage indicator switch
5. D.R. compass repeater
6. D.R. compass deviation card holder
7. Ignition switches
8. Boost gauges
9. r.p.m. indicators
10. Booster coil switch
11. Slow-running cut-out switch
12. I.F.F. detonator buttons
13. I.F.F. switch
14. Engine starter switches
15. Bomb containers jettison button
16. Bomb jettison control
17. Vacuum change-over cock
18. Oxygen regulator
19. Feathering buttons
20. Triple pressure gauge
21. Signalling switchbox (identification lamps)
22. Fire-extinguisher pushbuttons
23. Suction gauge
24. Starboard master engine cocks
25. Supercharger gear change control panel
26. Flaps position indicator
27. Flaps position indicator switch
28. Throttle levers
29. Propeller speed control levers
30. Port master engine cocks
31. Rudder pedal
32. Boost control cut-out
33. Signalling switchbox (recognition lights)
34. Identification lights colour selector switches
35. D.R. compass switches
36. Auto controls steering lever
37. P.4 compass position indicator
38. P.4 compass
39. Undercarriage position indicator
40. A.S.I. correction card hold
41. Beam approach indicator
42. Watch holder

The Bombing of Britain

The Blitz, Nazi Germany's sustained bombing of Britain, started 7th September 1940, though industrial targets in Liverpool and Birmingham sustained hits prior to this date.

The Blitz is automatically associated with London but Britain was attacked in very many other military and industrial areas. Barrow-in-Furness, Belfast, Birmingham, Brighton, Bristol, Cardiff, Clydebank, Coventry, Eastbourne, Exeter, Greenock, Hull (which was the most bombed city outside London), Liverpool, Manchester, Nottingham, Plymouth Portsmouth, Sheffield, Southampton and Swansea all suffered heavy casualties.

When the Luftwaffe concentrated on London initially the bombs fell on the Port of London but many fell on residential areas. London was attacked indiscriminately day and night from mid-September to mid-November.

By mid-November some 13,000 tons of high explosives and more than one million incendiary bombs were dropped.

On 29th December, in a severe concentration on London, incendiaries and high explosive bombs were dropped causing a firestorm that came to be called the Second Great Fire of London.

10th May 1941 saw the last of the major attacks on London, but it was perhaps the most catastrophic. There were more casualties than ever – some 1,364 people killed and 1,616 injured. Many important buildings were also damaged or destroyed and these included the Houses of Parliament and the British Museum.

It was now widely believed that we had no option but to 'fight fire with fire' and bomb Germany with more ferocity than employed to date, and less discriminately.

Coventry was deemed to be the second capital of England and had grown to become a huge industrial centre with engineering factories followed by munitions and armaments factories. Thus it became a prime target for the Luftwaffe. People were encouraged to leave the city for fear of attack and they left carrying and wheeling whatever they could. On 14th and 15th November 1940 Coventry suffered devastating bombardment. The city resembled an 'end of the world' film set, covered in rubble and bathed in dust, firestorms broke out and fires burned indiscriminately, smoke was everywhere. People in shelters struggled to breathe when the bombs were falling and many people smoked which added to the poor quality of the air everyone breathed. Over 500 people lost their lives and over 4,000 homes were destroyed. The once proud cathedral of Coventry that stood regally high over the city was virtually razed to the ground, but such was the spirit of the Coventry people that they were soon filtering back into the city and were calling for retaliation.

Such was the destruction that 'to be coventrated' became a new phrase.

Each bombed city was bathed in a grey blanket. Everything was grey. Depressingly grey. Grey was the colour of devastation and death but not of total demoralisation. British spirit only briefly flagged. British people remained stoical.

Hitler wanted to break the British spirit and bomb us into submission. It did not work; in fact it achieved quite the reverse. Britain was not demoralised, Britain was fired with a new sense of purpose, Britain would not submit, Britain wanted an end to the atrocities.

The Bombing of Germany

In 1941 Churchill said *"we need to make the enemy burn and bleed in every way"*

But even today the bombing of German cities remains a subject of controversy. It is however widely believed that the outcome of the war would have been very different if Britain had not retaliated.

Sir Arthur 'Bomber' Harris was in charge of Britain's bombing campaign and strongly believed that bombing less discriminately was the right course of action.

It was not until 1944 that Britain finally got the bit between the teeth and dropped the highest annual number of bombs on Germany. Targets were changed and railways, bridges and motorways were hit. Germany was virtually brought to a standstill by 1945.

Britain sustained an aerial bombardment of Germany from 1939 to 1945 and 61 German cites were hit during that time.

The delicacy of the subject of the bombing of Germany wherein civilians were hit, and the reluctance by many so to do, can surely be seen as an attribute of the British people. The fact that we still found that smidgeon of humanitarianism, even in the face of our own destruction, is surely to our credit. Unfortunately, however creditable this was, it would not have won the war.

Churchill told his cabinet 'the fighters are our salvation, but the bombers alone provide the means of victory'. Yet for all of that Bomber Command was the only unit effective in the war from 1939 to 1945 that did not receive a campaign medal.

It has to be recognised that air crew faced an inordinate amount of stress with each mission and faced just a one in twenty chance of returning alive on some missions. Casualty statistics were very high.

Many who survived became victims of the war and alcoholism and failed marriages also became more statistics of war.

Whilst most historical tomes list figures which can be boring in that they almost become insignificant purely because of the hugeness of the figures quoted, it is verily important to understand the vast catastrophe that is a world war.

There were almost 60 countries involved in the war and acceding casualties. The total number of deaths has been given at between 62 and 80 MILLION. We mourn the loss of our military personnel today in the wars that still, and probably will, always blemish our existence. In these wars the figures are running in the hundreds and naturally we are loathe to accept ANY of these deaths in a just and free world. Yet the Second World War decimated any acknowledgement that mankind was remotely man kind. With a population of over 47.5 million the United Kingdom lost over 385,000 military people and over 67,000 civilians. With a population of over 69 million Germany lost over 5.5 million military people and a variable figure has emerged of anything between 900,000 to over 3 million civilians.

These figures are too hard to comprehend. It is too hard to comprehend any war. To live in a war period was to live an unnatural existence and yet the resilience bravely exuded by so many is to be exalted.

The average sortie survival rate was just five sorties. Spanner did 33 but there were many who did a lot more. There were thousands who did a lot less through no choice of their own.

During the period of the war casualty figures were not something broached to any great extent. Nothing was encouraged to make people feel defeatist and that their efforts may in any way be futile. Churchill's orations were magnificent at keeping the British spirits up.

Operations

Spanner's part in the war was now being established. He was on operations and this was the process. Before every operation there was the briefing and this would happen a few hours before take-off. When a briefing was about to take place all the general phones were immobilised for secrecy. No outside calls were allowed under any circumstances and if a crew member had not said au revoir to his nearest and dearest then it was too late. Those flying would go in the briefing room and each crew would stick together when taking seats. There were many smokers and the room was soon enveloped in a haze of smoke. Everyone came to attention when the Squadron Commanders came in.

The target was displayed on a board, covered by curtain material until the optimum moment of disclosure to the ranks. Everyone carried maps and a huge rustle of maps ensued on disclosure of the target. The targets everyone liked least were Berlin and the Ruhr valley where the enemy defences were in greater concentration. Any previous attacks were discussed and what was known of the German defences. The reason for the choice of the target and its importance in the big picture would also be explained.

Next would be a board display of the weather forecast for the duration of the operation and expected weather fronts that may be encountered. Obviously cloud cover played an important part. Target timing and pathfinder targeting would be discussed and the colour of the flare for aiming point markers disclosed (this was changed for every operation). Information was given on weight of bombs carried (payload) and the frequencies to be used for the wireless operators.

Words of encouragement and a prayer finished each briefing.

Len says *"If it were to be a long flight many of the crew would take pills to keep 'em awake which the RAF provided. Then we would go and 'ave a meal, often bacon and eggs. After this we were now on operational standby and could not contact our nearest and dearest if we wanted to. It were a tense time waiting to go. Our crew tended to act a bit of tomfoolery and would sometimes be a bit jittery.*

Before take-off we all went to our crew room to get kitted up for flight. We all wore a conglomeration of things to keep warm, lots of layers including thick long johns. We all made sure we 'ad our very important lucky mascots., without these all would be panic as life or death depended on 'em. Our bomb aimer used to wrap a WAAF's stocking round 'is neck. I 'ad a lighter mi father 'ad given me. It were given to 'im by t'parishioners of Summerbridge and Hartwith Church after t'first world war and 'ad an inscription on 'presented to N.Watson after service in t'first world war'. I took that wi' me and allus kept it in mi pocket. I once lost it out of a train window in Darlington. We were stood in t'station so I got off and got onto t'lines and picked it up before t'train set off. It were a close thing, I wouldn't 'ave wanted to be without it.

Last but not least were our provisions. We were given wakey wakey pills, chewing gum and chocolate. I used to tek the chocolate 'ome to give to mi mother. Apparently some crews were given escape kits containing maps of Germany and France, local money, phrase sheets, compasses concealed in pens and buttons and a photograph that could be used in forged passports but I don't remember getting these. We 'ad to empty our pockets of other stuff and the things were put into numbered bags —one for next of kin in case we didn't come back and the other not for next of kin which were our general stuff for when we kem back.

When we went out to a flight we didn't move. If a mission were going t' be called off they would shoot a coloured flare into the air and the colour were changed for every op so that no-one could guess. Sometimes it were pretty cold just sitting around and we were over t'moon if one were called off and we went out for a drink then.

I allus did a final inspection before we took off. Skipper and I did final checks, we each 'ad our own checks and we both checked each other and repeated. DI's (daily inspections) were allus done by ground staff but I used t'walk round the aircraft anyway before gettin' in. When we got the order to go and the crew were on board, all the tomfoolery and jitters stopped because we were one unit working together and our jobs and training took over. We all knew we depended on each other and there were a huge amount of trust among us.

There were always waafs, groundcrew and airmen watching us take off and some waving handkerchiefs. I used to stick mi thumb up out of t'window. We never ever said goodbye.

Skipper allus called me Len or engineer. He 'ad a different name for t'other lads. He called em all sorts."

The control tower used to pride themselves on getting aircraft down as soon as possible because the Germans used to follow them back and try to shoot them down as they were going in.

"Once we were coming in and t'Skipper called up control lady to land. Rear gunner piped up 'oh let's get her in skip, she's only trying to be bullshitty'. Skipper gave 'im a right telling off and told 'im to be careful what he said as Skip might 'ave 'ad the tit button pressed (transmit button) which 'e 'ad and control 'eard it all. A message kem saying would flight Lieutenant Millington report to control, so rear gunner got played 'ell with again."

Specific Operations

These are just a few of the operations the crew carried out.

24/7/44 Operation Donges Spanner says *"the very first operation I went on we got 'it by flak. There were two screens in the flight deck one were on my side and the other were on the Skippers. A piece of flak 'it the centre piece on my side and if it 'ad been another two inches in it would 'ave come straight at me. Screen went off like a spider's web. Luckily it were made of some triple X stuff and it didn't come through. That were a nearish do and that were mi first one"*

25/7/44 Operation Stuttgart *"we were coming back over Stuttgart and the rear gunner spotted a fighter coming (Messerschmitts were now fitted with upward firing guns). He told the Skipper the area it were coming from and suggested which way to corkscrew. Skipper did it and only just in time, they 'ad cannons with tracers on and we only 'ad 303 machine guns. They went right past my window and just missed us"*

28/7/44 Operation Stuttgart *"we got coned three times one night on an op to Stuttgart. It were pretty scary to say the least. We corkscrewed and got out of the lights twice, but there were no sign of any target being lit up by path finders for us to drop our bombs on. Skipper said that if we got coned again we would drop our bomb load anyway, which we 'ad to do to get 'ome. I were a bit worried by this time about the petrol going down fast. We got coned again. We were well in Germany and we opened the bomb doors and dropped 'em. We also 'ad cans of incendiaries on board which 'ad to go. When we turned round for 'ome the rear gunner said that we 'ad started a hell of a fire down there. I 'ad a quick look and it looked like a whole street were on fire. We flew straight and level for a short while to enable the cameras to* *photograph and then 'eaded for 'ome. It broke daylight as we flew back and the Skipper told us we were not stopping up so high and we were going down to 'edge'opping 'eight (hedge hopping height). He dropped down so we were flying just above the trees and we flew at that 'eight over part of Germany and German occupied France. The Frenchmen were on their way to work and were getting off their bikes to wave to us. There were washing on lines and I said I could nearly nick some of it we were that low. When we got further over the channel the Germans opened up on us. They got the tail but they never 'it the gunner"*

On one particular operation Spanner says *"we got 'it by shrapnel over occupied France and I 'ad two engines that 'ad caught fire. When the first one caught fire I feathered it and then the second one caught fire. Oil tank 'ad been 'it in the wing and there were a sump in there that 'ad sufficient oil in it to feather the prop and stop it spinning. Anyway I couldn't feather it so the temperature were over the top and I 'ad no oil pressure. So I told the Skipper that the engine were going to cease up and the prop catch fire. At this point the Skipper gave us orders to put chutes on to bail out.*

The only thing I could do now were press the fire extinguisher for that engine which would spray metal bromide all over it and in order to press that button I needed both 'ands. I 'ad to lift a red tab and press the button and in so doing I caught mi rip cord and deployed mi chute. We were at about 15,000 feet and I didn't 'ave a chute. Flames coming out of that engine faded out as a result of pressing the button but I felt such a fool and obviously concerned. Skipper piped up that 'we are not bailing out, engineers lost his chute'. That engine kept spinning all the way back 'ome and the other two engines were going alright, but I never took mi eyes off those temperature gauges"

5/8/44 Operation to St Leddesseront *"When we were coming in to land I wanted us to do a belly flop but the Skipper said he didn't want us smashing it up any more than we could 'elp and we would land at the side of the runway on the grass. I told 'im that we 'ad lost the hydraulics and that I could lower the wheels with emergency air, but I couldn't lift 'em again as the starboard inner 'ad been on fire and ten to one that tyre would be burst. Skipper said that we would risk it."*

In an emergency a CO_2 bottle was used to lower the wheels on a Lancaster which just required a lever to be depressed to pierce it. Len did this but the red light remained on and it left them flapping and swinging with only one wheel effective. They came in to land on the one wheel but Spanner says *"I'll never forget that landing. The control tower were on that side of the runway and we 'ad dropped at about 90 miles an hour and started slithering and the people near the tower were off like a flock o' sheep!"*

3/8/44 Operation to Trossy St Maximin hit by flak, hydraulics U/S. *"it were Wittering where we 'ad done our emergency landing and afterwards we wandered round the airfield looking at all the planes that 'ad crashed. It were 'ard to tek in"*

4/8/44 *"On return to base another Lancaster came in to tek us back to RAF Balderton and then we 'ad to get into another Lancaster immediately, start up and fly around for a while, this were to stop us losing our nerve"*

17/8/44 At this point F/Lt Millington was made up to Squadron Leader and moved from 49 squadron to 44 Rhodesian squadron. 44 was Denholme Lodge but was moved to Bardney and the crew moved with it. They wanted experienced crews for pathfinding and they volunteered so went to Spilsby temporarily.

9/9/44 Operation Munchen-Gladbach *"One op we were sent on was to Munchen Island which were an island just off the Dutch coast. Two squadrons were briefed to bomb two gun placements. One of these were on our starboard side as we were going in and the other were inland with a farm'ouse stuck up out of water. Munchen Island 'ad been flooded and it took 'em years to drain it apparently. Anyway our target were the one inland. When we went in I could see the other squadron bombing on the coast on mi starboard side. We couldn't find ours even though we flew round three times so the skipper sent the rest of his squadron home telling them to return to base. We too set off back home but we turned round and went back at 'edge 'opping 'eight* (hedge hopping height) *and managed to find the target and drop our bombs, but they opened up on us and we were 'it with two cannon shells. I knew we'd been 'it on the port wing and the port engine caught fire. When we got back the plane were written off.*

Once we were just about to go on our bombing run and the Mid Upper called on the intercom that there were smoke coming up into 'is turret. I folded mi seat and climbed up over the main spar and went down the fuselage. I got on mi knees and could see that there were smoke coming out of the floor. Bloomin' 'eck, I thought, the bomb bays are under there. So I went quickly back to mi position and knelt on t'floor by the steps down to the nose. There were a little door which I could open and look into t'bomb bay. I looked in and all the bombs were on fire! I switched microphone on to t' Skipper and asked 'im to open the bomb bay doors and let 'em go. It were quicker for 'im to do it than me as he had a lever at side of 'im. That were a close call"

30/10/44 Operation Walcheren. *"We were 'it by flak on this op and unfortunately rear gunner got wounded in both legs.*

We even went on a Dam Raid – the one we did burst the side walls in daylight"

Len on leave with his beloved dog Trixie

Home on leave again with Newby, Trixie, Leonard and friends

Sadly LMF

Darmstadt. There was a very sad incident that upset the crew while they were flying over Darmstadt. They had released their bombs and were caught in heavy searchlights with flak bursting all around. It was so close that they could not only see and hear it but could smell it. The skipper carried out his evasive manoeuvres of throwing the plane around the sky whilst trying to keep on course for home. Spanner says *"It were pretty 'arrowing when we 'ad to do this and I saw the navigator Jimmy getting up and saying he'd 'ad enough and was getting out of 'ere"* Jimmy had 'lost it' and he gave his charts to the skipper. *"The skipper got Scotty the bomb aimer to take over as he 'ad some navigator training"*

Jimmy had suffered what others had and could no longer cope. With the pressure of being under the almost constant certainty that death was a whisker away, he had cracked. This condition unfortunately was called LMF – Lacking Moral Fibre. The skipper did not really have much option but to report it and Jimmy had to suffer the consequences. The skipper said in his book that he had expected a medical investigation into Jimmy's condition but that was not to be the case. Jimmy was stripped of his badge and rank. The skipper said he would have recommended extended leave in the hope that Jimmy would recover his nerve rather than report him if he had known what would happen. He said he had rarely had so much sympathy for someone's plight and remained angry that he had been unable to foresee what would happen to Jimmy. He last saw him in a dirty uniform cleaning toilets.

"Jimmy were part of the crew, 'e cracked under the pressure but 'e were still part of the crew and our lives had depended on him just as much as the rest of us and he remains an 'ero in my eyes"

The term LMF was a grossly inappropriate title for what can only be described as a medical problem. The army had an even worse term of 'cowardice in the face of the enemy'

The air crew had to concentrate hard on their jobs to try to block out the reality around them. It is hard to comprehend the relentless and loud droning of the engine, the lit sky with flak bursting all around knowing these are shots aimed at you, seeing another aircraft getting hit and wondering who is going down or even knowing who is going down. Worst of all was the fact that the aircraft had to be flown steady, straight and level for a length of time when approaching a target knowing full well that you were presenting a perfect target for the enemy. When 'bombs away' was given and the aircraft shed its load the aircraft would significantly react from being lighter and so did the mood of the crew. They were not out of the woods yet though. Enemy aircraft were known to sit in cloud above English air bases waiting for aircraft to return and they unleashed their fire on them there. Many aircraft were actually lost over England.

Being sent night after night out to bomb people and try to survive being shot at was relentlessly robbing them of their bravado and youthful hope and the belief in life that is the right of every young person. Is there no wonder that it broke the spirits of some?

Spanner says *"I were twenty two when I finished bombing Germany"*

10ᵗʰ September 1944 Le Havre
Joe's Story

O ver the years Spanner met up with many who had taken part in the war. One man was Joe Hardcastle, a fellow dales man.

Joe Hardcastle was one of three dales men who joined up and travelled together to Strensall Barracks on the 15ᵗʰ February 1940. Against all the odds they all came back from the war.

Joe spent sixteen weeks at Strensall and then he was transferred to Stobbs Camp at Hawick to join the 1ˢᵗ/4ᵗʰ Battalion Koyli. Next he was sent to Greenock to join the RMS Andes bound for Iceland. 'B' company, of which he was part, was based on the east coast at Seydhisfjordhur and their mission was to prevent the Germans taking it and using it as a 'U' boat base. He spent the better part of two and a half years here where boredom was paramount and not alleviated by the odd scare of a 'U' boat sighting or lone enemy aircraft. He did however get some valuable training in winter warfare and became adept at living out of doors in arctic conditions. This did not go without its perils though as there were eight fatalities on one training exercise.

After the Americans took over in August 1942 the Battalion moved to Ross-on-Wye. Training continued and in July 1943 they were moved again, this time to Crieff to do combined ops training at Inverness and Rothersay. They were eventually moved to Lowestoft for yet more invasion training.

Action was about to ensue and they were taken to Tilbury Docks and onto a ship on D-Day. The following day they anchored off the Normandy beaches and were met by the most spectacular sight which

Joe will never ever forget. There was such an Armada of ships and boats that it was impossible to count them and there was floating rubbish everywhere. He had never seen such an inhabited seascape of flotsam and jetsam in his life and fervently hoped never to see the like again. On the beaches were wrecked landing craft, and abandoned transport and tanks. It was a desolate and dispiriting sight.

The Luftwaffe tried to bomb at night and the sky was lit with tracer from hundreds of ships. This too was a spectacular sight and the service he remembered being held on board with 'Abide with Me' being sung did nought to lift their spirits.

His Battalion landed in Normandy on June 10th and the next day they took over in the line of advance. Battle could be heard being waged in the distance. They attacked the village of Cristot and then they progressed to Tessel Wood which was taken and held for three weeks. They proceeded on to the Caen area, where they encountered a new enemy – mosquitos' by the hoard. These were intent on having a feast at their expense but their spirits were high regardless. The scenery had changed somewhat and instead of the dead men, dead cows and wrecked tanks and vehicles left by the Germans they encountered villages intact, with food, wine and pretty girls much in abundance. When they arrived at the Seine they found equipment and stores of every kind including vehicles and horses.

They went over the Seine to Le Havre which was a strongly fortified port. Twice the Germans were asked to surrender. There was a cease fire wherein the Germans came to HQ under the white flag but they refused to surrender on both occasions.

It was at this point that the RAF was summoned to add air support to the army's endeavours.

Guess who was flying in that air support – yup, no less that Spanner himself.

Len couldn't help but say *'if I'd known you were down there Joe I'd 'ave dropped a bomb on you'*. Joe could have retorted something about the accuracy of bomber commands aim, but he didn't. Len and Joe had a friendship that survived over the decades.

The RAF went in with heavy bombers on three raids and Joe says they all had a grandstand view of this. Then, at dawn one September morning, the Battalion attacked and by afternoon the Germans surrendered – over eleven thousand of them.

This was not the end of Joe's work as the Battalion had to continue but at least there was no shortage of food and drink for them now. They went on into Belgium and on to the River Maas. Joe remembers it was 5th November because the town of Klundert was ablaze from end to end. The Battalion then progressed to Nijmegen and Arnhem which had been flooded by the Germans and they spent an uncomfortable winter patrolling it. Then they progressed to clearing Dutch villages however the enemy had fled from these areas.

On V.E. day Joe was in Ede where there was nothing to drink but tea! They then went on to Utrecht where they received a great reception. They spent all of the following week disarming Germans. In April they went to Meschede in Germany where a small group supplied the needs of displaced persons.

Joe went home on leave in November, had his appendix removed and went to Halifax convalescent depot, and then he was demobbed at Fulford Barracks 8th May 1946.

Joe says *"It seems a long time ago, but how well I remember the comradeship, the laughter, the tears and the courage of the lads fighting a War they did not want, not forgetting the lads who did not return. The gory details of which there were plenty, have been left out. For the infantry man there is no glamour, war is a horrible experience"*

* Courtesy of Joe himself and the publication 'Upper Nidderdale in Uniform' by Swires & Hardcastle

Pathfinding

The RAF wanted experienced crews for pathfinding and Spanner's crew volunteered and they went to 44 Squadron.

Spanner says *"After we 'ad gone to 44 Rhodesian Squadron we got a weekend pass and because we were expecting to be posted to a pathfinding unit we put our log books into the flying office before going. This were because you 'ad to 'ave your log books signed every month by the CO. When we went back we found out that there 'ad been an op and a Lanc. 'ad taken off and a tyre 'ad burst and it went through the flying office and there were a lot of damage. We 'ad to go to stores and get new log books and thus lost our training time that were logged in the old books. The new log book continued till we finished. That's 'ow I managed to finish up with two log books because the first one were eventually found".*

In November 1944 the Skipper was made up to Wing Commander and became the CO to 227 Squadron at Balderton and that's where they were posted to.

"He never went on all ops so I were a 'spare' and the flight engineer leader Colson were a 'spare' too. I 'ad a desk in 'is office and if 'e were flying as a 'spare' I weren't. I used to check the logs for the following day to find out if I could sleep in or not. I 'ad to go see the skipper every morning and report as 'e relied on me for looking after the rest of the crew. One morning the flight engineer leader told me there were an op on that night and they wanted a flight engineer 'spare' and that 'e 'ad already done three 'spares'. I told 'im that I 'ad also done three 'spares' as I'd done a third with the skipper. He went through the list and said there were a sergeant Shaw who had now done three ops and should be capable of doing a 'spare' and his skipper is sick so won't be

flying. So I rang up t'mess and asked for Sergeant Shaw and asked 'im if he'd like to go. He said yes. He never came back".

After this they went to Spilsby as a staging post before they told them where they were going to be posted to that weekend. "*After that, because we didn't 'ave addresses, we just shook 'ands and said we'd see each other when we got back*"

They never saw each other again.

Burma

Sadly Spanner never did go back or get to see his comrades again. He was due to get six months rest period at the end of his tour and while he was on leave he received a letter advising him that he was going to be posted to Catterick.

His leave was probably the one of the quickest six month periods ever and he was very soon at Catterick and being told he had to have yet more tests because he was an ex.fitter. He was then given three choices on what to do next – either back to basic trade as a fitter, Transport Command or British Overseas Airways. He opted for British Overseas Airways but got Transport Command and was posted down to Abney. He was crewed up again and he went on a glider snatching course. This was with a view to rescuing wounded forces from the jungle.

Spanner says *"The Dakota 'ad no door on it and I leaned out of this to snatch. We practiced on wagons. The winch were on t'bottom of the wagon and the driver would drive like the devil to the perimeter and we would fly past to snatch it."*

That sounds quite dangerous to say the least.

"glider snatching were quite a change. My job was 'andling the winch which were in the aircraft. It consisted of 14 steel plates all clamped together with springs. I would put brake settings on and then wind the handle on the winch anti clockwise to tek it off. I would drop the rope and the ground staff would signal what weight I were pulling off. We flew down very low above the ground and we snatched gliders out at 90 miles an hour and mi guts went into t'back of mi body every time! To set up a snatch we didn't 'ave a door on and I used to 'ave to 'ang out of the aircraft like they do in 'elicopters to set the

lower arm. The wire rope kem down a chute and then through the door onto an 'ook. It 'ad a dove tail tram line which were threaded on the top and then below 9' with a fisherman's gaff, which I 'ad to push down onto a retaining clip at the bottom. Then I would tell t'skipper I were ready to snatch and then the ground staff would put two poles up 9' high with a circular rope. Then we would snatch the aircraft. The first yard of that were a third of the thickness for a failsafe so that if it were going to break it would break there. Initially the gliders were towed into the jungle, which we sometimes did, and they would release themselves. The gliders were not like the gliders that can be seen nowadays at gliding clubs, these were big aircraft that were like 'ospital wards and could bring out a lot of wounded"

The Dakota was an extremely strong aircraft and for training purposes they did blind flying *"there were a pencil gong over a map next door and I've landed under the ground many times with one of them!"*

It was quite an experience for Spanner in Burma. He had to get used to eating pretty quickly as others did not fare so well. There was a huge variety of different insects and animals to contend with. The houses were built on stilts because there were lion eating tigers roaming around. He says *"That put a bit of wind up us"*

Len and his comrades enjoy an Eastern pint

Where we lived

In transit through the Suez Canal

Boat Spanner built out of a tank – but forgot who the chap is!

Spanner was posted to India next to Petang aerodrome at Chittagong and he remained there until the bomb was dropped on Hiroshima. They did a lot of flying and transportation of equipment. He remembers finding an old motorbike on the airfield and fixing it up. He and his comrades had a lot of fun with that bike.

He was then moved to Rangoon and he was given a room above some law courts. He says *'The war were more or less over other, but the Japs were still at it a bit'*

He had an interpreter and they travelled into the jungle together looking for crashed aircraft. The last position each aircraft had was indicated on a map and they would search in this vicinity and then on to the nearest village.

"We employed bearers to carry a bit of stuff for us. We went through jungle fire at one time which weren't a lot o' fun. In the villages there were stages and villagers sat on t'floor. We slept on a stage and there were a crypt in one corner on this stage and we kept looking at it. I found out that there 'ad been two

missionaries and one couldn't stand it so 'e went 'ome and t'other one stayed. There weren't any telephones or owt like that but there were jungle telegraph. Runners used to run between villages and they knew we were coming before we got there.

I remember once being in a village and we were sat in an 'ut and one of the old men were watching us. Well I got out one of mi not-very-pleasant anti malaria tablets and put it in mi mouth to swallow it; we all carried 'em. This native saw this and 'e put 'is 'and out for one. Well I didn't 'ave the 'eart to refuse 'im so I passed 'im one. This man didn't 'ave many teeth and 'e chewed away on this tablet like 'e were in a best gurning competition and we 'ad to try very 'ard not to laugh but when 'e 'ad finished 'e put 'is 'and out for another one!

We were once looking for a Dakota that 'ad crashed in the jungle and we travelled over 1,000 miles in a jeep and then walked 30 miles to get to it. A missionary had gone to a village nearby and he walked to meet us because 'e 'ad buried the occupants of the aircraft and wanted permission to move them to 'is own chapel in 'is village. I can't remember what the outcome of that was.

The missionary 'ad formed a band that 'e 'ad taught 'imself and 'e brought 'em out. They 'ad whistles of different sizes they 'ad made out of bamboo and they played Home Sweet Home for us. I were well put out because I didn't 'ave mi mouth organ with me, I would love to 'ave played with 'em. 'e wanted me to write to 'im after the war but I lost 'is address.

We travelled a bit up into the 'ills above Mandalay and it were so far up it made the jeep boil. The interpreter introduced me to 'is brother who lived up there. 'e were an unusual 6'4" and were a Captain in the guard and I got friendly with 'im. We did manage to mek quite a few friends out there.

I were later introduced to a jeweller, Mr. Durri, and I 'ad my 21st birthday party at 'is place. I allus remember it because I 'ad a few RAF lads there. Mr. Durri said seein' as it's Lens birthday we'll ask 'im to say grace. After a bit of rapid memory searching I said the one we used to say at school and got out of it that way! We played lots of games and one I still remember were really quite daft but it made us laugh a lot. We would get 'old of a piece of charcoal and then each of us in turn 'ad to say the following without laughing – I 'Leonard' *hath no spots, 'ow many spots hath thou o – and if we laughed we would get a black mark on our faces. We managed to get covered in charcoal and laugh our socks off and that were without any alcohol!"*

One specific thing that happened in India was they had taxi'd the plane near to a tent as they had to get a lot of passengers on board assisted by ground staff. The crew had a drink of tea and then prepared to fly out. When they took off the skipper said *"there's something wrong here, have you put the rudder locks in?"* To which Spanner replied *"no because there is no wind"* The rudder locks were literally two pieces of wood with elastic between which were placed between the rudder and fin to prevent the rudder blowing backwards and forwards when there was a wind and thus reducing the air pressure. It was only used when there was a wind. The navigator piped up *"I put rudder locks in Skip"*. The Skipper gave a painful glance at Spanner and said *"I am going to turn it round and go back in"*. The Skipper took a very wide sweep round and phoned ahead to say they were going back in as they had forgotten something from the tent. Luckily the Skipper managed to handle it right and when they landed Spanner shot out of the door and ran to the tent pretending to collect this phantom 'something' while the rudder lock was removed. If they had not done that the navigator would have been court martialled.

Spanner and comrades relaxing in the mess in Burma
In the very formal the Squadron HQ dining area

Waiting to service

Squad dining

Formal dining

Posh mess dining

Spanner enjoyed his time in Burma and it provided him with rich memories. He had to consider his future now that the war was over and he had to consider his family. His parents had supported him fully, if not wholeheartedly, throughout the war but he knew how much it was upsetting his mother now that he was so far away and not totally out of danger. She used to send him letters very regularly and she was very pleased when he decided to leave the RAF.

He was demobbed Warrant Officer Leonard Newby Watson service No. 1533108 on 30th April 1946 with effective date of release 18th August 1946. In five short years he had already experienced much more than most do who live long lives and he was only 24 years old. In his Service and Release book it states he received the France, Germany and Burma Stars, the defence Medal and the 1939/45. Also hand written therein it says 'A hard working, keen type who excels himself in motor mechanics'

He was afforded a travel warrant to get home and the obligatory outfit. This was a suit which was not of poor quality, coat, shoes, socks, shirt, tie and underwear. Now he was supposedly equipped for life in Civvy Street.

1946 Farewell Dinner with menu typical of the day. Soup was the usual starter and a main course was usually meat and two veg. with 'brown' gravy. Woe betide it be any other colour. The duck is an added surprise. The dessert was again a usual choice. Wobbly blancmange was heaven.

WARRANT OFFICER
WATSON.

48 Squadron's Sergeants' Mess.

Farewell Dinner.

18TH. JANUARY 1946.

W/O Hartry. S/Sgt. O'Shaughnessy. W/O O'Kane. W/O Holme.
W/O Ledora. W/O Nield. W/O Allen. Sgt. Harnett.
Sgt. McLeod. Sgt. Buckmaster. F/S Weeks. Sgt. Clark (651)

Sgt. Thorburn. Sgt. Davis.
Sgt. Keogh. F/S Brierley.
Sgt. Kirk. Sgt. Benner.
Sgt. Hoy. F/S Christie.
F/S Cook. W/O Daldorph.
F/S Millar. W/O Dunne.
F/S Speak. W/O Elliott.
W/O Hobbins. W/O Goodwin.
W/O Fell. F/S Gilford.
W/O Toyne. Sgt. Partridge.
W/O McManus. F/S Higham.
W/O Stirrup. W/O Hodgeson.
W/O Saxton. Sgt. Keen.
F/S Winkworth. W/O Humphries.
W/O Rigby. W/O Lake.
W/O Ross. F/S Madely.
W/O Baker. W/O Martin.
W/O Basten. F/S Maxted.
F/S Crawley. W/O Pope.
F/S Farley. W/O Powell.
W/O Berein. F/S Reid.
W/O Wensley. W/O Rogers.
F/S Brown. Sgt. Clark (524)
W/O Bultitude. W/O Roome.
W/O Lewis F/S Andrews.
W/O Bailey. W/O Armstrong.
F/S Ball. W/O Ellinor.
W/O Faber. F/S Higgens.
F/S Lloyd. F/S Martin.
F/S Hagger. F/S Neal.
W/O Grant. W/O Rees.
F/S Bardsley. W/O Rushmere.
W/O Brewer. W/O Todd.
F/S Crawley. F/S Sabine.

W/O Seal. W/O Seymour. W/O Stabler. W/O Thompson.
Sgt. Summers. F/S Thornhill. W/O Tillion. W/O Turner.
W/O Watson. F/S Watts. F/S Myring. Sgt. Wise.

Menu.

SOUP.
CRE'ME TOMATO.

ROAST CHICKEN.
ROAST DUCK.
ROAST POTATOES.
GREEN PEAS.
CAULIFLOWER.
STUFFING.
BROWN GRAVY.

DESSERT.
JELLY, BLANCMANGE.
FRUIT & CREAM.

BEER—MINERALS.
CIGARETTES—CIGARS.
FRUIT & NUTS.

PATENGA. S·E·A·A·F.

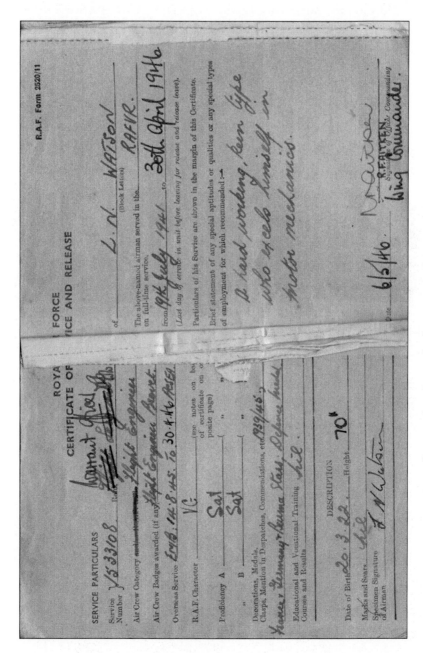

Spanner's release Authorisation August 1946

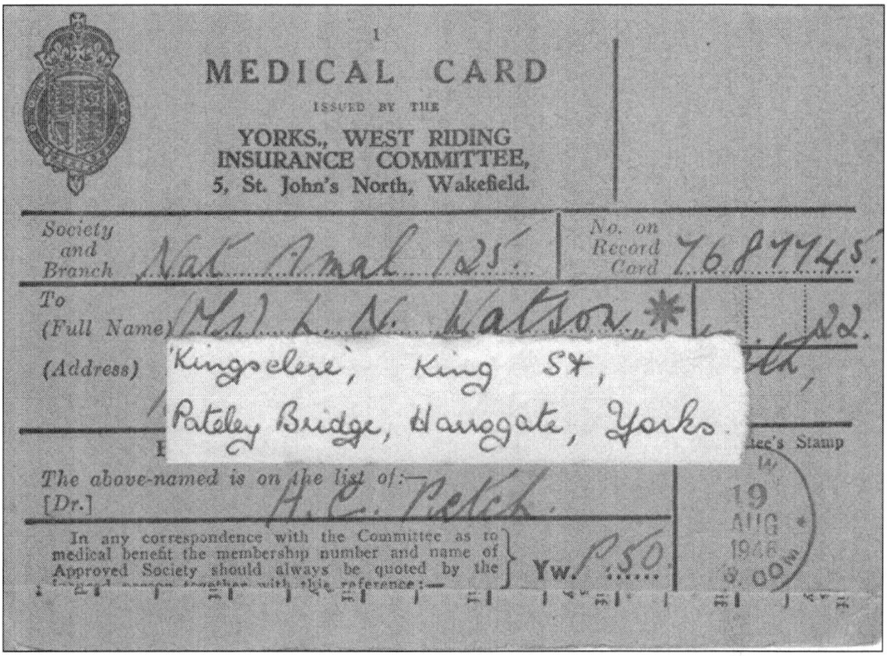
1

MEDICAL CARD

ISSUED BY THE

YORKS., WEST RIDING
INSURANCE COMMITTEE,
5, St. John's North, Wakefield.

Society and Branch Nat Amal 125.

No. on Record Card 7687745.

To (Full Name) Mrs L. N. Watson

(Address) 'Kingsclere', King St, Pateley Bridge, Harrogate, Yorks

The above-named is on the list of:—
[Dr.]

In any correspondence with the Committee as to medical benefit the membership number and name of Approved Society should always be quoted by the

Yw.

19 AUG 1948

Medical card

Home Again

Leonard now relinquished his Spanner moniker and became Len Watson again. But what Spanner had experienced was well and truly in his blood and his none defeatist attitude and predilection towards repairing, constructing and sometimes inventing were to mould the rest of his life.

He had to think about his future and he gave serious consideration to both his skills and a possible career where it was likely to be most lucrative. The main areas were either vehicle maintenance, from his now not insignificant mechanical background, or the construction industry from his days in joinery and building. There were many men being demobbed who had mechanical experience but a lot less with construction backgrounds, so that was the trade he decided to enter.

Len went to work for Dick Andrews in Dacre. Dick had a funeral directors business and making coffins was Len's main occupation but he also learnt the undertaking business. Dick eventually decided he wanted to sell up and Len had saved a bit by now and he bought the business from him. Just after he bought the business he also got registered at Lawnswood as a building and civil engineering contractor and received a certificate which was dated 1948.

While all this was going on he was also building his social life. He liked to play darts and he used to go to the Bay Horse at Burnt Yates for a drink and game. His brother had a friend called Frank who lived locally and one day he asked Len if he fancied coming with him to a dance at Moorpark at Beckwithshaw. Len had enjoyed dancing very much so it didn't take much persuasion. Len had a Hillman car and he knew that Frank was after a ready lift, as he was courting a girl called Barbara who was a land girl, but he didn't mind as it suited them both.

Moorpark was where a hostel was for the Land Army girls.

Miss Wright

Len says *"One Saturday night some Land Army girls wanted to go to a dance at Huby so my car were full of land girls, not a bad thing I thought at the time. Only problem were mi dynamo 'ad gone off charge but I thought it would get me there and back. I got as far as Beckwithshaw then it wouldn't start again. I asked if there were any way I could borrow a battery and one of the girls went and asked the forewoman. She lent me a battery off one of their pickups and she sent word down that I must 'ave it back by Monday morning. I promised I'd fetch it back even if I 'ad to get a taxi to bring it back.*

On the Sunday I took mi battery down to Matt 'ousemans and got it charged up and sorted out the problem with the dynamo. I took the other battery back to Moorpark on Sunday night. Barbara went to tell the forewoman and she said to put it back on the van and mek sure it starts, which I did"

Well that was that or so Len thought. He went with Frank to another dance and he pointed out the forewoman to him. She was dancing with an army officer from Pennypot at the time. Eventually Len asked her for a dance and got the chance to thank her for the loan of the battery. Her name was Betty Wright *"and that was the start of the rest of mi life!"* Len said.

Betty was in the land army for a while and had spent some time in a village called 'Kingsclere' in the south. She was then sent to Beckwithshaw and eventually became a forewoman. When a land girl got made up to fore woman she was expected to move to another group but the girls didn't want this and set up a petition so Betty got to stay.

Len and Betty now started seeing each other regularly. She used to take the wagon down to Harrogate (Arrigut) and she parked it in the station car park, so the girls could go to the pictures with their boyfriends. Len started going to the pictures with her. That was the start of their romance.

There were no driving tests then and the wagon Betty had to drive was quite large. She did get used to it but that was after she took a bicycle out of the hands of a poor soul pushing it up a hill. Because of this she was eventually required to take a driving test. Len didn't have to so never did.

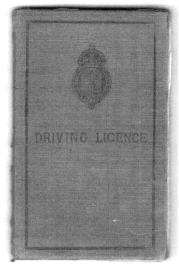

Driving licence cover

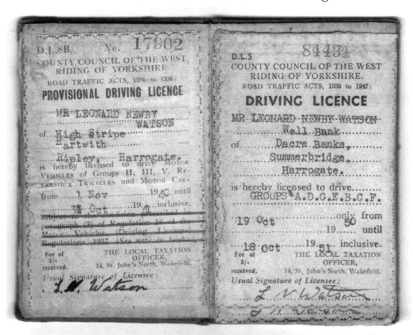

Len's driving licence from 1940!

Miss Wright – pretty as a picture

The Land Army girls – Betty is third from right

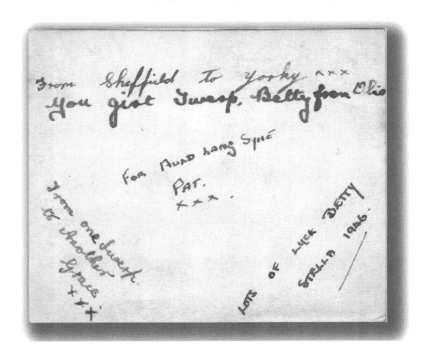

Len and Betty were getting on so well that he asked her to marry him. He doesn't remember the actual asking, only that she said yes. They arranged the wedding to take place at Beckwithshaw on 31st May 1947. The land girls formed an arch holding up spades when they came out of the church. George Lumley, Len's long time mate, was his best man.

As a special gift Len gave Betty a heart he had carved from the perspex from an aircraft canopy and he had mounted aircraft wings and a crown.

Wedding Day with land girls

Newby, Jenny, Bert, Len, Betty, Pat (Betty's best friend and Maid of Honour), George (Len's best friend and Best Man), Betty's mother Alice and Betty's eldest brother Dick.

Len says *"The wedding day oh it were a good 'un. I've allus said I were christened by a canon, married by a canon (Canon Peck) but the Gerry's canon missed me. The canon fire went straight passed my window. By I were lucky, we all were"*

The wedding reception was a meal provided and held at Matt Houseman's farm with the family in attendance. Len and Betty went on honeymoon to Scarborough for a week.

"when we kem down to breakfast the following morning who should be sat at the only other occupied table in the room but our local doctor, Dr. Petch. We said it weren't everyone who took their doctor on honeymoon with 'em"

When they got back from honeymoon they moved into a wooden bungalow that Len had managed to get. He had got two to choose from but he took the one that was nearest to his workshop in Dacre.

"We moved into t'bungalow in Smelthouses and within a few months Betty became pregnant and a year later on 9th June our first born Gillian were born"

Hooray it's me, I am here, and I can talk now – even though my memories don't really kick in for a few years yet. And now Len's name has changed again – to Dad this time.

After another year Dad had a chance to buy a house at Dacre Banks which was just up the road from his workshop.

This is probably their first invoice, written by Mum and sent out just 14 days after I was born.

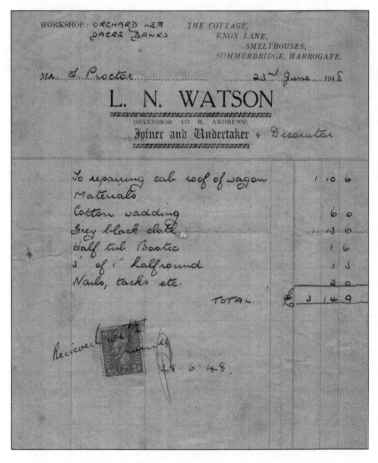

First invoice

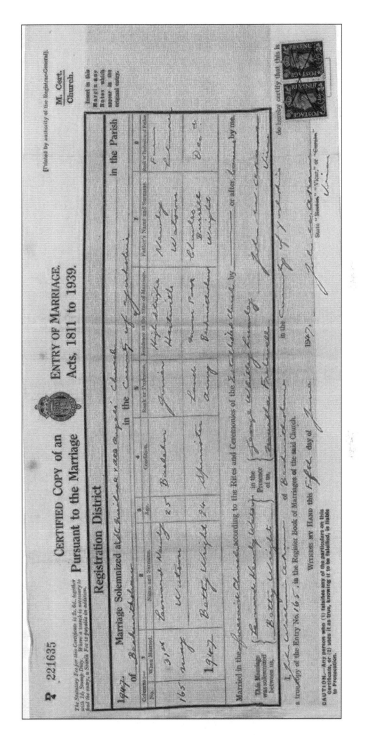

Marriage certificate

101

Dacre

For added confusion 'Leonard' aka 'Spanner' is now Dad.

We moved to Dacre in Summer 1949. Dad moved all our goods and chattels in his van. The house was on the hill on Dacre Banks conveniently just up from his workshop.

Dad says *"I got a bit of a rude awakening when I found out that we 'ad to 'ave Betty's mother living with us in the summer time. She spent winter living with Betty's elder sister in Reading, so she were with us 'alf a year each year and I 'ad to keep 'er"*

Dad doesn't remember anything about the move only that the house lent itself readily to providing more workshop space. There were four houses in the row with a garage in the middle which belonged to our property. There was also a two storey lower ground floor part to the building built at right angles at the back of the property. Thus we had a workshop at lower ground level that was approached through the garage, and a store room and paint store at ground level off the back passage. With a living room, front room (not called a lounge in those days), and four bedrooms the property was quite substantial. There was also a glass lean to at the back and a separate outside toilet.

The house had no kitchen to speak of and there was no running water when we moved in and Dad had to go down into the village with Laddie and carry water up from the bottom of the hill twice a day from a pump which is actually still there. That pump is now a land mark in the bottom of Dacre.

"when we 'ad a funeral in I could start making a coffin in the morning, run 'ome from mi main workshop for mi dinner at 12 o'clock, run back and I

would 'ave the coffin finished, lined and polished with all the metal furniture on by tea time"

We did not see too much of Dad because he was always working and didn't have any men to start with at Dacre. He often worked at night and would often stop at the Old Oak or the Flying Dutchman in Low Laithe for a pint on his way home.

"ee, I remember it used to tickle me that there were a bloke in Low Laithe who used to grow cabbages and stuff in is garden and then sell 'em to 'is wife."

The well visited pump in Dacre village

Gill's early memories of Dacre

These are my specific memories of Dacre I was too young to remember Smelthouses but Dacre was special.

In May 1950 my sister Janis arrived followed in October 1951 by my brother Terry.

I loved all the nooks and crannies of our house even though it was cold. However I didn't like having to go to the outside toilet. It was spooky. It was in the back, concreted, yard and down some usually damp steps. It had two wooden toilet seats in one room. One was our toilet and the other belonged to Mr & Mrs Geldart who lived next door. What an innovative idea. Needless to say both toilet seats were never occupied at the same time. They had buckets underneath and the council emptied them for us. We had to use a polly (potty) in the house at night and I used to check under the bed for bogeymen before I put my feet out in the night if I needed to use the polly. I definitely believed bogeymen existed. Probably still do today.

Dad put a water tank on the roof of the paint shop and we had running water at last. Mum used to spend a lot of time washing in the glass lean to at the back. She had a single tub that had an agitator in and a rubberised ringer on top, but prior to that she had used a tub and a dolly.

One day Dad, in his wisdom, decided to put an old bicycle tyre on the fire in the living room. In those days you always burned what you could to keep heat going. Unfortunately he had forgotten the tyre had metal coiling in it and it sprang out of the fire splashing burning rubber all over. Jan and I were in stages of undress, I still had my dressing gown on but Jan only had a vest on and got splashed. She bears the scars today.

Because there was only two years between Jan and I whenever we got presents bought we tended to get the same things but in different colours. I remember wanting something different even if it cost less. Even our clothes were the same and the same colour sometimes.

Christmas was brilliant at Dacre. Santa Claus used to put out presents in individual pillowcases. One present I got was a three wheeler bicycle.

Dad says *"I 'ad crept into Gill and Jan's bedroom to put their presents at the end of their beds. Gill, always the nosey one, woke up and I got stranded. I 'ad to wait ages to creep out again. But it didn't stop there as just a short while after I got back into bed all we could 'ear was a flippin' bicycle bell being rung – at three in the morning!"*

For one Christmas present Dad built Jan and I a rocking horse which used to swing a bit like a plank swing. He had painted it and put a piebald effect on it and red shiny fabric seat. Apparently he was up until the early hours on Christmas Eve finishing it. I remember sitting on it with Jan.

Rocking horse with Grandma Wright and Laddie with Jan and Gill astride. Dad built it so well that it was apparently still in use over fifty years later, albeit somewhat tarnished through loving use.

Dad says *"Laddie were a grand dog but he were a bit of a roamer. When 'e got back I used to say 'where the devil 'ave you been' and 'e would show 'is teeth at me and it got to be a game. I used to do it with 'im when I took 'im to the pub. The lads used to say that 'e would go for me yet but 'e never did. I just used to pat mi leg and he kem to me wagging 'is tail"*

Christmas presents usually consisted of a painted tin of mixed toffees which I loved, a pack of 6 bath cubes which I did not, a tin of talcum powder which I loved, a jig saw which I soon got bored with, a box of hankies with flowers in the corner that we never used or a painting or drawing book which I loved. I particularly loved the magic painting books and the tracing books. The very best things were the comic annuals. I would read every inch of mine and then start on Janis and Terry's. Sometimes there would be a game of snakes and ladders or ludo or tiddly winks. I preferred some of Terry's presents though because he got mechanical things like a painted tin wind up baby dipper (small big dipper or roller coaster as they are now called) – much better than girly presents. Mum and Dad always put our present in individual pillow cases placed around their bedroom so that we didn't get mixed up and there was always an apple and orange at the bottom. When you got down to the apple and orange you knew you had run out of presents. Mum used to make us take our time so she could write down who we had got what from so that we could write our thank you letters. Woe betides us if we did not write our thank you letters. There was only so much you could say about how wonderful bath cubes were.

We used to have quite a few family get-togethers at Dacre whereby aunts, uncles and cousins used to come and visit us. Mum's brother Uncle Stan used to come with Aunt Doreen and cousins David and Christopher from Leeds. We once decided to go as a huge family entourage down to the river to swim. Uncle Stan was a very good swimmer and would swim with various children on his back. On one occasion we even had Grandma Wright in tow. Well after the swimming we decided to continue along the river bank with a view to walking up through the fields back to our house. We children were all for it as it extended our outing. We trudged up through one field and into another. This second field was a pretty large one and in the topmost corner was a cow. Except it wasn't a cow, it was a bull. By the time the more discerning adults had decided this was the case we were all beginning to get a little nervous of our position particularly as this bull was giving us remarkably undivided attention. A decision was made to evacuate the field which resulted in a dramatic and ungainly scramble over a high wall. It was an unseemly display of tough male talk and flapping female skirts. We children thought it was hilarious. Still don't know whether it actually was a bull but it made for a lot of laughter.

A favourite picture

*Jan, Me, Terry and Mum and 'Old Jowett van' outside
Dacre Banks house*

Holidays

Holidays were not something Mum and Dad had contemplated in the early years and with three small children and a business to run the coffers were a bit empty to provide for them. However, Dad put his Spanner head on and had yet another one of his bright ideas. He had put together a metal tubular frame to sit on the back of his big (well it was to us) lorry to cover tools and building materials in transport. Now what if ….. This 'what if' became a grand master scheme to have a family holiday. The idea was that we would ALL go on holiday and ALL sleep under cover on the back of the lorry. The ultimate in innovative holiday accommodation.

Meantime, back in my head, I had decided I wanted to have a holiday elsewhere. On School Lane, just up from our house, there was a youth hostel and I was fascinated by the fact that people came and stayed there. It had a big room with beds in – a bit like an old fashioned hospital ward. That's where I wanted to have my holiday. I asked Mum if I could stay there for a week instead. Ah. Mum told me that's fine but that would mean I would have to stay all on my own while they went on holiday to the seaside and had fun. Big decision for me and I deliberated long and hard. I think Mum was impressed that I did not decide straight away. Well guess what I decided – the lorry trip of course. But that was before the plan was thwarted. Janis, in her wisdom, got Chicken Pox the night before we were due to go. Oh I was mad and I blamed her for spoiling our holiday as if she'd done it on purpose. She had of course I knew it.

Aha. So now I could go back to plan A. I could go to the youth hostel. Wrong. The scheming of a seven year old got shot down by the adroitness of adult mother. I was told I could not go on holiday if we all could not as it was not fair. Doubly Janis' fault! I marched around with the proverbial pet lip for a few days on this one. Hence I have never forgotten it and Jan thinks it's amusing. She is so right. Damn.

Grandma Wright, Mums Mum, was with us each summer and she was a bit bossy. It seemed a bit unfair to us because we had three bosses – Mum, Dad and Grandma. She used to do a lot of knitting and I remember some windjammers she made us. Naturally Jan's and mine were matching.

We three were just little children at Dacre but I am left with some of the fondest memories.

I used to be fascinated by the train that ran between Pateley Bridge and Harrogate under a bridge that was half way down Dacre Hill. It was a steam train and very noisy. It used to stop at Dacre station which was just by the bridge and when it set off again the whistle would blow. Whenever I heard the whistle blow or heard the train coming I used to try to run down to be on the bridge when it passed under, that way I would disappear in the smoke that would billow out each side and over the bridge totally obscuring it. I never did quite make it but I was once walking up the hill when the train signalled to set off and I ran and caught the last dying remnants of the smoke. That taught me a lesson. I coughed myself silly all the way up the hill.

Who can forget those first magical years of life?

Modernisation

The big 'L' shaped room off the back passage slowly became established as the 'paint shop' (as opposed to work shop) and got invaded by half empty paint tins, left over wallpaper, idle paintbrushes languishing in foul looking liquid and various rags in various stages of variable colour composition. Very messy. We were supposed to keep out. Ah, yet another rule to be broken. Well we were not that bad but we did push it a bit.

Dad decided it was high time we had a 'proper' kitchen. This was huge excitement for us but it did seem to take forever for him to do it. It was a good size room and the back part was made into a dining area with windows that looked right across the dale to the 'top' road. I often sat there to paint, draw and scribble. The view was brilliant and something Dad often reminisced about after moving from Dacre.

It was after this that the lean-to at the back door was demolished but I think we used it as a playroom for a time.

Life Defining Moment

In the small back room at the end of the passage from the back door Dad had decided it was high time that he installed a bathroom. To our small minds this was excitement beyond anything. To actually be able to have a bath in something that fills itself and empties itself AND to be able to do it without anyone watching was wonderful. The best bit of all was not having to use the polly (potty) anymore and not having to go outside to that ominous and slightly intimidating dual toilet down the steps in the back yard AND to be able to do a wee in the house. Bliss.

Up until this time we had bathed in a tin bath in front of the fire in the living room taking it in turns using the same water which had to be manually filled, or we had a strip wash standing up in the square sink in the corner of the living room when we had running water.

Dad still chunters to this day about having to carry that water up from the village pump. Such trials and tribulations.

This small back room was covered in one of those 'period' linos and had various items stored in there. One day, while I was day dreaming about this new bathroom that was to be, I decided to go and look at the place where the toilet was going to be. Then I thought I would pretend that the toilet was already there so I sat down on the floor, but I didn't stop there. I wanted to feel what it would be like so I took down my panties and I thought I could just do a little wee and pretend the toilet was already there. Then Mum came in and caught me.

Ouch.

I got my first 'I want the ground to open up and swallow me' moment, but it was to be a long time before I would know that sort of vocabulary as I was only four or five years old.

Mum pulled me up and I remember saying "I was just …." And Mum said *"I know what you were doing"* and she called me a dirty girl. *"I was going to clean it up"* I protested.

Dad didn't know any of this and it caused him huge amusement when I told him. Tis good to make one's Dad laugh.

Our neighbours had a bathroom and after ours was put in, Dad decided to fill in the area of the old toilets in the yard. This left a hole with boulders in. A rat appeared one day so after a good old scream from us Dad came out to investigate. He then proceeded to kill the rat with a clothes prop. Spanner to the rescue again.

Terry however has never been forgiven, oh no, there's nothing like a grudge. I was on my three wheeler bike one day and he was in his peddle car and I asked him to give me a push, so he did – straight down the hole. I only got a grazed ear but about the same time Jan was in a field and fell and broke her arm. She had a propensity towards breaking her arm. Terry of course has never been forgiven.

The Business

Dad started to take on more work not just in carrying out funerals but joinery and building. The first apprentice he took on was Alan Holmes whose father was the baker at Summerbridge. Then he took on another joiner Frank Dean followed by Terry Thorpe (Terry T. from hereon not to be confused with my brother) who became Frank's apprentice. He also took on Jack Richmond for building work.

I felt quite proud that my Dad had men working for him, even at that young age. I used to love watching the men work and I thought they were very clever. I watched Terry T. and Frank make coffins many times and was quite fascinated by the grooves they put in and then bent the wood to form curves. The finished result was polished and had metal handles and a plaque and was quite beautiful. I watched Terry T. in later years wallpapering, when Dad finally got round to letting them actually work on our house that is. All outside work had to come first. It was a case of 'cobbler's kids'. I have actually wallpapered 26 rooms in my adult life – all from watching Terry T. I think I had a bit of a 'hero worship' thing on him; he laughed a lot and was lots of fun and of course clever.

Dad was always out working. Mum was always home working. It was much more time consuming in those days to keep a house and run a family.

One thing they did for us that I treasured immensely was they had comics delivered each week for us. I got the Beano, Jan got the Dandy and Terry got the Topper. I charged down the stairs on comic day. I read mine voraciously, then Jan's and then Terry's but I did think Terry's was a bit childish. I read all the Christmas albums we got. I did all my painting books, magic painting books, stencil books and tracing books then I would start on theirs if they hadn't bothered with them. That was the best thing about having siblings – three of everything.

As I got older I used to play cards with Mum and Grandma a lot, particularly canasta. We used to laugh a lot together.

Grandma used to have All Bran for breakfast with glucose powder on, which we weren't allowed to touch. So I did. As you do.

Parochial Hall

The Parochial Hall stands at the bottom of Dacre hill facing the village green. This building was the focal point for all village activities. Major Hirsch used to take the Remembrance Day parade but Dad did it once when he was abroad. They would march from the Hall through the village and on to Dacre Church.

I remember going in there with Mum and a cacophony of voices and footsteps on the wooden floor. We queued up for provisions but I cannot remember what for exactly. All I know is that we had to do it regularly. This was the rationing that still went on after the war finished.

Sweets were not something that we were used to. Mum used to buy a Mars bar and she would slice it in small pieces and we were allowed one piece. Oh how we loved Mars bars. Nothing gave me greater pleasure as I grew older than to buy a Mars bar and bite all the chocolate from the outside until all that was left was the limp inside. It took ages to eat it that way. I am sure the chocolate was thicker in those days.

I remember having sugar sandwiches when I was very young. They were quite gritty but we loved them. I remember Dad having lettuce chopped up with sugar and vinegar on. We thought it was very grown up but again I liked it.

At school I was introduced to the delicacy of school milk. This was our wonderful government's way of ensuring all children got extra vitamins and hopefully not get rickets. Why was it always warm and unappetising? The local tiny sweet shop used to sell straws that had a small piece of felt in them which was soaked in fruit juice. This made our school milk more palatable. Other sweets we could get in those days were liquorice, sugar mice, sherbet dabs, cinder toffee, fruit gums, Spangles, fruit Polo's with a pull tag to open them, Smarties, compressed fruity icing lollies, dolly mixtures, toffees, gob stoppers and, if you were lucky you got one with a black centre. Kaylie was lovely, you could buy it loose and eat it with either a stick of hard liquorice or dip your own finger in which invariably turned red. Lucky bags also came out around this time and would usually have black jacks or fruit chews, a plastic toy and a few gums in them. Chocolate slowly developed into very different forms and one of my favourites to eventually come out was the Nux bar which was rather like the Lion bar of today. And sin if all sins dolly mixtures are not the same any more.

Dacre boasted two shops Jacksons and Skaifes, one leaned towards being a general store selling most things and the other leaned towards green grocery. Now there has been a demotion and only one store survives.

The Parochial Hall held many activities including regular jumble sales. Major Hirsch's wife held an annual jumble sale which I think was for charity. The standard of jumble was however very good and this occasion drew huge attendance from all over the dale. It was a major event on the calendar and queues started forming well before the doors opened.

There was a band that used to play regularly called 'The Victoria Band'. The players were a goodly collection of local musical talent – there was Mrs Proctor on piano, Ronnie Swires on saxophone, Kit Abbot on trumpet, Arthur Braithwaite on drums with Bill Abbot taking over the drum spot, and last but not least Millie Walsh. Now Millie was a character and she had one gold tooth that she flashed regularly as smiling was something she had perfected for her stage performances. The best bit was she played with gusto and she always wore stockings which were held up by garters; the more she played her 'squeeze box' the more her stockings wrinkled down. Needless to say all eyes were not on the playing.

Whist drives and domino drives were often held there and Dad says *"Jack Gill and me used to tek 'is radiogram into the hall and teach the kids to dance"*

Another thing the Parochial Hall had that I found fascinating was it had a room on the back with a flat roof on with a paddling pool on top. I desperately wanted to paddle in it so I asked Dad about it. He said that I couldn't paddle in it as it was to collect rain water.

Oh! I thought, understanding fully not at all. Eventually they removed the 'paddling pool' much to my dismay.

Parochial Hall today, somewhat spruced up now renamed Dacre &
Hartwith Village Hall
On the far right is the building that had the 'paddling pool' on top

Dacre Fete

Fetes were held on the village green in Dacre bottom by the Parochial Hall. The green is triangular in shape with a stone seating area at each corner and still presides over Dacre today. Little side stalls were set up on the green including the mainstay of village fetes – apple dunking. I only tried it once and had to cheat a bit to push the apple to the side of the tin bath to get a tooth hold. The fun was in getting wet. Then getting covered in sawdust and wood shavings after dipping into the bran tub for the lucky dip. Dad supplied the sawdust and wood shavings of course. All kids loved the lucky dip. I would do it today given half a chance even in my ripe years! Sawdust of course would be a Health & Safety no no. Spoilsports.

Fancy dress processions used to progress around the green and sometimes along the road. Materials for fancy dress were not widely available and parents 'made do' with what little they could either afford or get. For one particular fete Mum sorted two different outfits for Jan and me – but of course we had to have the usual coin tossing operation to decide who wore what. I think it fell pretty much fifty fifty over the years but I won this toss. Mum had some random pieces of patchwork material that she put together and swathed me in – thus I became the rag queen – she even made a ball of something to signify an orb to carry. Jan got stuck with being a mini painter. An old painters pinny and an over large white coat was wrapped round her, a flat cap placed on her head, a paint pot in one hand and a paint brush in the other. She was not amused.

Another village celebration was on Coronation Day in 1953. Again Jan and I were dressed up. I lost the toss this time and was dressed as 'winter' thus I had to wear my pinky red mackintosh with the hood up and wellies – on a warm day. Jan got to wear her swimsuit as 'summer'. I seem to recall pretending I didn't care – stoical to the end. We marched round the village green and along the main road towards Summerbridge culminating at the Max Pullan cricket field in Summerbridge bottom. The Max Pullan building still exists and used to have a covered seating area, which has been long since enclosed for cricket/ football changing areas.

The playing fields are used often today and hopefully will remain so.

This is the priceless photograph of Jan and me on that 'I am not amused' day. Her expression is magnificent. Over the years she perfected that expression and one always knew when she was not amused.

Gill Starting School

I started school at Summerbridge at the same school Dad had gone to all those years ago. I quite enjoyed school and I remember trying to do 'joined up' writing, where you wrote a constant squirl along a straight line. I also remember painting a picture of a little girl but could not get the feet right and had them sticking out at right angles, but the teacher thought it was good and put it on the wall. What an accolade.

The school was perhaps just over a mile away down the hill, round many bends and 500 yards on a lane running by the river. This seemed a long way for a five year old. I was allowed to have just one way bus fare so it meant I had to decide whether I walked to school or from school. Children were so much safer then than today. Parents would not dream of sending young children to school unattended now. It is such a shame that life has become so precarious now. The decision was however taken from me as I had to avoid the 'stone throwing' little boy who lived in Dacre bottom. So I preferred to walk to school but if we were running late it meant I had to take the bus and run the gauntlet coming home.

I remember once Mum had got some 'special' balloon stuff in a tube. You had to put a nob of this on the end of a straw and blow it up. The result was a fairly see-through but tacky balloon. I was fascinated and wanted to be very clever and turn up at school with one of these. Mum told me it might not survive the journey to school but she indulged me and blew one up for me to take. I had to get the bus, as the balloon would probably burst if I walked, so I waited at the bus stop just across the road from our front door. The bus came down the hill and it did not stop, blasting down the hill causing a great wind swirl in its wake and whipping the balloon out of my hands. I was dumbstruck, distraught and dumfounded. I am sure you get the picture. I know Mum did because she was watching at the other side of the road and when the bus passed I saw her looking at me so sad. She knew she could do nothing to alleviate the situation and that I had to set off walking to school without my precious balloon. Mum gave me a hug and I know I wanted to be a big girl and not cry but it didn't work. I didn't really do the 'pet lip' thing but I reckon I must have had one on for the whole of the walk to school that day. I didn't like bus drivers after that.

I saw some of that substance Mum made my balloon of quite recently but have no idea what it was invented for in the first place.

There was however a bus conductor who was pretty cool (not that I knew that word then). He took a liking to me and called me Sunshine (which I did not much like to start with because I had already named one of Mr. Lambert's cows 'Sunshine'). This cow was probably the one that scared the wits out of 'our Jan' one day while we were standing on Mrs Braithwaite's steps next to Mr Lambert's field. The cow came over and we were patting it but then it put its tongue out and licked Jan. Well cows have huge long tongues and wow did she scream. I thought it was hilarious. We were very good at laughing at each other's misfortunes.

We loved it when the feast (funfair) came to Dacre bottom. We always had to win a goldfish. I really hated cleaning their water as it did not smell very nice. Whatever happened to all the goldfish we won over the years I do not know. They must have passed on and surreptitiously been removed from our sight without our knowledge. Clever people – parents.

Bonfire night was another to remember. Dad had, in another innovative moment, decided to erect a paint shop in the back garden, on our 'bit' as opposed to Mr and Mrs Geldart's 'bit'. This was a wood and metal construction with no attractive qualities and did not please the aforementioned neighbours. However it stayed for quite a long while. When it finally came down we had a bonfire on bonfire night. Dad was lighting fireworks and one chased me all over the garden following my trajectory. It was a 'plane' firework that was designed to fly. We also had jumping jacks, which were concertina folded and, when lit, on each turn of the fold they jumped – in an erratic manner. This was very scary for young children. This is one item I am quite happy that 'Health and Safety' have banned.

They were good early years. From pinching apples that hung over Mr Bundle's wall onto our property (and some that didn't) and to playing doctors and nurses and using plants for dressings. To poking the water in a trough on School Lane to see if the newt would show itself and to talking 'turkey' talk with Mr. Lambert's turkeys. I am pretty sure the turkeys understood everything I was saying to them.

Spanner's at it again

Changes inevitably invade the halcyon days do they not? So it was to be. Dad's business was progressing well and he saw a bigger and brighter future that could not be conducted from where we were.

Mum and Dad checked out many properties and through one of his men, Jack Richmond, he learned of a property in Pateley Bridge that was for sale.

Off we trotted for the 'family' property check out. I was nearly 8 years old by now and not overly happy about any change nor were Jan and Terry I think. Apparently we three ran all over this new big house and then eventually I had said 'can we go home now?' little knowing that 'Kingsclere' was to become our home for very many years to come. I remember the smell of the property and thinking it was a nice house and newish and I remember picking up an old penny off the floor.

We moved to Pateley to this 'big house' in 1956. The house had a long skinny kitchen with a cream Aga at the end and over it one of those clothes airing racks that hang from the ceiling that you lowered to hang your washing on. There was a food hatch to a square dining room which was a vital link not just in serving family meals but in communication. The dining room had a fancy red-bricked fireplace and the lounge had a smooth stone fireplace with stone matching shelves each side.

Dad says *"we did miss the view that we 'ad at Dacre. The Pateley 'ouse were flat in the valley but it were a good decent sized 'ouse. I 'ad to think about equipment and tools for the future as we 'ad much more workspace. I 'ad a Universal but it weren't fast enough for t' circular saw but too fast for t' planer, so I got individual machines. I 'ad a twelve by seven thicknesser planning machine and a separate circular saw. Then I got an electric mortise machine and a big band saw. I were well fitted out"*

Mum eventually bought a full set of Encyclopaedia Britannica to go on the shelves in the front room. I was in heaven. These encyclopaedias became my tomes and were well leafed through. There was so much information and I particularly liked the poetry bits.

There were 4 bedrooms which were a godsend as little did I know it but my siblings were to be vastly increased in quantity over the coming years.

Now outside, well that was another story. Loads of outbuildings – all specially devised to challenge enquiring minds. Opposite the back door was a smallish room with an 'L' shaped room behind it. Dad decided hens we would keep – so hens we did keep. I think we did get some eggs from them but they were never really successful, just a bit smelly. The smaller room became our next childhood campaign. *'Can we have a play shed Dad, please, please, please'-* beg beg. He couldn't help but crumble under the onslaught of three small children pleading a case so vehemently. We got our play shed. I think I spent most time in there of the three of us over the years. It was once a school room with desks in, then a living room with soft chairs in, then an animal welfare centre. I raised pet mice in there at one time. And gerbils took house briefly on school holiday from the school they were residents of and needing looking after. The stick insects Ella also offered to look after, much to Mums discomfort, took up residence in a bedroom.

I took my mice out for a bit of fresh air one day and let them roam on a raised clothes horse quite firm in the belief that they couldn't get off it. Then I forgot about them, had my tea and eventually went to bed. Then I woke up in panic. Mum and I went searching the garden in our dressing gowns making silly squeaking noises, to no avail. Never did get them back. They have probably fathered/mothered a whole succession of several generations possibly prolific in the dales now.

As usual Mum couldn't get home improvement work done in the house. Cobblers kids again. She wanted the dining room decorated and the walls were left stripped forever and a day. Mum eventually got so angry that she painted and drew things on the walls. One said 'this room needs painting badly, and even badly would be better than it is now', another was a drawing of a tin of paint and 'Rembrandt' written alongside, there were several others. As we got many visitors, particularly sometimes possible customers for dad's business, he got shamed into actually decorating so to this extent Mum's artistic impressions worked. Hah. But when Dad finally did get around to decorating it caused much mirth as all Mum's artistic efforts were visible through the new decorations.

'Kingsclere' after the front porch was added on

The yard

Terry aged about 12 years standing in yard

Jagger's Bungalow and Others

One of the earliest buildings Dad had to construct was that of a bungalow at Greenhow for the Jagger family. The site chosen had no services but there was a deep well.

Spanner to the rescue. His idea this time was to tap the resources of the well. The well however had to be inspected and rendered out. This meant he had to get a man down the well. Now here's to the big idea. He took the children's garden swing which was on chains and he put it onto the digger shovel. With Ken Batty sitting on it he swung it over the well and lowered him down into the well. Ken actually did the pointing in that precarious position. Hard hats – what were those? Health and Safety hadn't been thought of. But they managed it.

The bungalow is still there in a very open and windswept area.

One of the very first jobs they carried out at Pateley was building a bungalow at the end of Millfield Street next to his property for Mick Williams. They also carried out many barn conversions over the years as well as new builds.

Dad was getting quite a lot of funerals to carry out then and it helped carry the firm while he took on the larger jobs.

Dad says *"In the early years we built council 'ouses up Hartwith bank which Jack Richmond did most of as Ken were on a job at Hampsthwaite doing a farmhouse extension. We also built some bungalows at Summebridge. It were about this time that I bought a JCB and started taking on water mains work"*

The firm did a huge amount of work in the dale, not always on time, as some dales folk would certainly say. Keeping work flowing was a hard task and Dad knew his men's livelihoods depended on this as well as our own of course.

There was a period whereby much of the work was barn conversions and this brought many others into the dales. Moneyed people started to come in and there was even the odd helipad constructed.

Thruscross

In the 60's water was becoming a big problem and the reservoir capacity for the Leeds area was not sufficient and had to be addressed. So it was that a site had to be found and a new reservoir had to be built.

Thruscross became the fourth reservoir in the Washburn valley. Like many reservoirs before this there were buildings that would have to be submerged in the process. The tiny village of West End lay in the bottom of the valley though it was more or less vacated as a result of the decline of the flax industry. The village did however have a church and permanent residents who needed the required respect afforded them before any flooding could started. Many graves along with headstones were relocated to a small graveyard on the Greenhow Road.

It was now that Dad got the calling. More literally he got a call from Leeds Church Commissioners who wanted him to build a new church. This was a huge undertaking for Dad as there were no services to the site on the hill that was to be used. He had to bring water from the valley in a trailer he designed especially for the job.

He was also given the task of removing the bell from the old church to be re-sited in the new church.

Again he put his Spanner head on and he took Edwin and Peter to help him. Dad and Peter went up to the top where the bell was and he asked Edwin to hold the rope to lower the bell. When they were supposedly in control of it Dad went off to get something. It was not one of his best ideas. Edwin left the ground still attached to the rope. Dad grabbed a bit of the rope and burnt his hands hanging on. They managed it in the end and the story became a source of much amusement.

They also took on the job of removing the leaded lights. This was a huge job as they were of significant weight.

Thruscross reservoir was completed in 1966. A sailing club subsequently took up residence and they used to tell a lovely little story to visitors that Dad's aforementioned activities unfortunately put paid to. They used to relate that if you came on a windy day, and days are often windy up there, and stood on the shore in as close proximity as you could muster to where the village had been, you would hear the church bell ringing. Some believed this and swore they heard it but any noise they heard had to be attributable to the waves lapping the shore line. No bell no ringing.

The new church was an incongruous monolithic blot on the landscape. The design was abysmal and not thought highly of by the local community. It had an inverted roof with one part being approximately half the length of the other. It was a modern intrusion in the middle of a beautiful and sparse landscape. What were they thinking of. Needless to say the building is no longer used as a church and came eventually to be used as a hostel and outdoor centre.

The new church – what were they thinking?

Thruscross Church

Memorial Hall

Mr Kenyon, an architect, asked Dad to put in a price for building the Memorial Hall in Pateley Bridge. Others had also been asked but had declined. The construction of a hall was causing a great deal of controversy among the townsfolk and ill feeling was in abundance. Even the men who worked for Dad were not convinced it was good to take the job on and thought it was too big a job for a small firm. Dad took it on regardless of the local discord and work began in earnest and took a while to complete as it was a building of considerable size.

Sadly feelings ran so high that Dad was not even invited to the ceremony of laying of the foundation stone. He was quite upset about this at the time particularly as they had done an excellent job of the building.

Just as things are today when change is imminent people will come out of the woodwork to object and often without foresight. The Memorial Hall proved to be a big attribute to Pateley Bridge becoming a focal point and venue for a myriad of events over the years. Jan and I have both appeared in productions on the stage there and the local youth club met there for a while. Whist drives too were regularly held. Many dances were hosted and even rock band gigs were staged. More lately there have been antiques fairs and sales.

This was back in 1959. Grandad Watson (Newby) still worked for Dad and he worked on the hall. I used to go see him and he always carried mint imperials with him and that tempted us children to go see him. I thought the world of him and I don't think I ever heard him raise his voice.

There was a time when Mum and Dad considered emigrating to Australia but Grandad had a stroke so they decided against this. I often wonder what would have happened if we had emigrated.

The Memorial Hall half built

*The ceremony of the laying of the foundation stone in 1959.
I remember grabbing Mum's old camera and running on to King Street
to take this picture.*

(See colour section – The Memorial Hall today)

Two Generations of Children in Same Family

My earliest memories revolve around Mum and my next two siblings. Dad was always working so we tended to only see him at mealtimes. There was quite a gap between us three and subsequent four children. So it was Me, Janis and Terry. Janis decided she wanted to be called Jan when she got old aka 'grown up' but she was Janis or Our Jan' then. Terry and I were 'Our Terry' or Tus and I was 'Our Gill'. All my siblings were given second names except me. There was a family who lived on School Lane and they had two daughters Mary and Janice. Both were older than me – Janice was the youngest and seemed to run a lot, Mary was older and went to school on a bus in a uniform and I thought that was special and clever. Hence I renamed myself Gillian Mary Watson. Whosoever asked my name was dutifully treated to the full moniker. I was later told that, although I did not have a second name, I was the only one that was planned. I thought their planning was ultimately pretty suspect.

At the tender age of 16 years I remember walking with Mum on to the High Street to get some shopping. As we were walking I tentatively broached a subject that was bothering me. I said *Mum are you pregnant?* – she said she was. I was quite annoyed and said *'not another one'* and *'couldn't you have told me I had to find out from someone else'* – I thought I was a 'grown up' then. I had such a long way to go. Little Paula came along just before my seventeenth birthday. I sometimes tease Paula and call her 'not another one'

Our Janis was my next down sibling so naturally we argued and fought as children. Janis was quite good at turning on the tears thus she tended to get Dad on her side. I was always able to win in a 'talk fight' and I would think before lashing out. Jan would wade in with flying fisticuffs but I would tend to land only one clout which brought on the tears. So Jan would win because Dad scalded me. It took me a while to work it out. The two years between us was a lot when we were children. As adults we went off and did our own thing with our lives and now get on pretty well and don't do fisticuffs anymore.

Our Terry was 'slap 'appy' as Dad used to say, and this pretty much summed him up. He was a lot of fun and got up to japes. He was a happy child and played with Meccano a lot building some pretty weird contraptions – like father like son. Unfortunately he had to carry the 'I want my only son to follow in my footsteps' thing from Dad. Dad did tend to let him 'get away' with things and Terry learned to milk it and grin at us when Dad wasn't looking. Terry in his teens developed a bravado bordering on dangerous, mainly to himself.

Butter wouldn't melt

Me, Terry holding Ella, Marie and Jan sitting on a brown leather backed sofa in 'Kingsclere' lounge. We had gone up in the world as 'the front room' had now become 'the lounge'.

There was a big gap between Terry and Marie so we were rather like two generations of children in the same family. I was the eldest of the first set and Marie was the eldest of the second set.

Dad never did learn that it was better to love, nurture, guide, teach and sometimes chastise your offspring but not expect them to adhere to what you want of their lives. Love us – yes he did in his own way but he didn't do cuddles, nurture – he provided for us extremely well, guide – he told us what to do, teach – again he told us what to do, chastise – he was quite good at that. He did however amuse us whenever he had the time. A favourite was when he used to put on his much revered and tenderly brushed funeral top hat. He would stand or sit against a wall and put his finger in his mouth and blow his cheeks out. Whenever he did this his hat would rise at the front. He had us totally convinced it was magic – for a short while.

To Dad Terry was always the important one as even then times were still very male dominated. He wanted his son to follow in his footsteps and thus much was expected of him. We were unaware of the pressure this put Terry under. We mere girls were expected to do regular chores from which Terry was totally excused. Janis and I, as the elder two, had a regime to follow of washing up and cleaning. We had to take turns 'doing the pots'; one washed and the other dried for evening meals and weekends alternating the jobs on a weekly basis. We also had to clean the lounge and dining room in turn on Saturdays and Sundays. We had to clean the Chapel of Rest sometimes and once I even had to do it while there was occupancy, prior to the visit of a mourning relative. Yep we knew our place. Strangely I am not complaining that is just how it was. I used to get very frustrated as all I cared about was getting my chores done and getting out to play. Jan on the other hand took her time. Thus I finished up more often washing up rather than drying just to be able to get out (escape). I just adore my dish washer now.

As Marie and Ella grew older they too were issued with household chores. Particularly after Jan and I got married.

Three eldest .....

Me, Terry and Jan in the garden at Kingsclere. We used to spend a lot of time in the Recreation Ground (Rec) at Pateley Bridge around 1958/59. All local children spend a lot of time in the Rec. In those days we had a big slide, not like the paltry little one in existence now. Health and Safety has taken the fun away from so much. 'Us kids' did alright without them running interference!

Four youngest .....

Top to bottom – Marie, Ella, Lynn and Paula on the front garden at 'Kingsclere' – this would have been about 1967.

Our Marie was born in 1957 and she was adventurous, wilful, stubborn and always missing. As a small child she was not into being hugged or picked up like adults tended to want to do as she was pretty cute. She took to escapism in the literal sense. When she was a toddler we older kids (Yorkshire for children) were constantly being told 'go look for Marie'. It got to the point that I used to think 'why can't we just leave her lost and then we don't have to keep looking for her' I thought that was pretty reasonable.

Her escapism was put into full swing when she was only a toddler. She would get out of the garden and disappear. The garden had a high wall down one side that she could not get over but a low wall on the other, so Dad put a length of chicken wire down this side. Marie in no time at all sussed this new challenge and buried under the wire then over the wall – goal achieved. Dad reverted to type and on inventive mode he put a washing line the length of the garden, he then put a ring on this with a further length of string attached to reins and these in turn were attached to Marie. Voila! She could go the length and width of the garden without escape.

This was short term because she had the audacity to keep growing and subsequent escapism was much more effective. She used transport.

As a mere whipper snapper (Yorkshire for hyper child) she went down the lane to the bus station and got on a bus. The conductor couldn't see her as she was so little and only found her when the bus had left Pateley. All Marie could say was 'I'm going to see my Grandad.' Our Grandad lived a few miles down the dale and Marie was on a bus going up the dale. They had to take her to the end of their journey and bring her back. The conductor walked up our lane with her. Meantime we were all running around like headless chicken looking for her – again.

She did it again. This time she got on the school bus going up the dale again. Because it was the school bus no-one realised she shouldn't be on it. She got off at journeys end – Scar. She went to the bungalow of Dad's friend John who played with him in their dance band. There was no telephone and Johns' wife, Barbara, had to wait until John got home to take her back to Pateley. Again we were all out on the 'look for Marie' mission.

She was quite artistic as she got older but this started with forays into the art world fuelled by tomato ketchup and vim on the hall floor. They would probably be masterpieces now.

Our Ella came along two years after Marie in 1959. She was a very pretty baby and developed into a bright spark and was always mischievous. A local girl, Barbara Goddard, used to take her out in her pram. She took her all over and they ultimately became lifelong friends. When Ella was young I was busy being a teenager so spent little time with her.

They loved playing in the sandpit, as did all of us. Subsequent generations of grandchildren also got wind of this fun-to-be-in spot. Making dens at the back of the buildings was an absolute must for all of us. Pinching putty from the joiners shop to use as plasticine was a nightmare to Mum who had the task of removing droppings from the carpets. A builder's yard was perhaps not the safest environment for little children but we all had a lot of fun in it.

Marie and Ella used to argue a bit and got up to a bit of mischief as did Jan and I. Christmas of course was ripe for mischief. They too liked to search out, prior to Santa Claus visit. Marie did take advantage of her older status and cajoled Ella to sometimes take a risk on her behalf and would send Ella in to do the 'scouting'.

They had one memory that makes them laugh today. Apparently Ella woke Marie to say that she thought Dad was killing Mum! Marie charged downstairs to find out what was going on. Dad, as usual, had come home late and they had started arguing and Mum had lifted her stick and said *"I could hit you"* Dad had then said *"go on then"* He got himself so worked up he put his face an inch from Mum's —and stuck his tongue out. They then fell about laughing. Marie casually went back upstairs and told Ella it was alright as it was just Mum killing Dad.

Marie, apart from being stubborn, was also very loyal and definitely had a 'no fear' attitude even from a young age. Dad in his infinite wisdom had let a local man keep an old vehicle in the yard but he had to ask him to move it when he decided he wanted to make another entrance into the yard. This man did not want to comply with this reasonable request so reason went out of the window. Dad advised him that if he did not move the vehicle then he would get his JCB out and dump it outside his house. They were arguing and Dad was in the JCB and this rather large man was climbing onto it. Marie to the rescue! She promptly ran inside and got her hockey stick, jumped on the wall and wielded it at this large man threatening *"I'll bray you over the head"* Threats were in abundance. Mum however was standing in the window laughing at the lot of them.

Our Lynn was born in 1962 and was a darling. When she was small I was working for Dad in his office and thus at home in her early years and for that I am very grateful as I got to spend time with her. As a very young baby she developed pneumonia and was so poorly the doctor thought she was not going to make it. There was a point whereby she looked so ill he expected her to go and Mum picked her up and colour came back into her. The doctor said he wouldn't have believed it if he hadn't seen it. Lynn was funny and came out with some corking statements. She could light up a room just by smiling. She did however have one annoying habit that Dad gave up on trying to change. She used to drag all sorts of items from the yard onto the lawn and build contraptions. A climbing frame thing was one, and another was a sort of see saw. We used to watch her engrossed in making these things and she became our floor show. Dad could not stay mad at her for long. Some of the things she built would doubtless today be classed as works of art.

Our Paula was a very quiet soulful child. Poor thing was afforded the luxury of being given a second name by me. This was to appease me for Mum and Dad having the audacity to have yet another child. I remembered a picture of a quite beautiful actress in my 'Girl' diary named Maxine Audley. Paula thus became Paula Maxine Watson. As she grew up she was not impressed. Now she thinks it's 'pretty cool' – she's an American now and that's how they talk.

By now Dad had become a bit of a 'cuddles' man purely because Paula gave him no option. Mum's health had been poor for many years and she was poorly for much of Paula's childhood. Paula took to climbing on Dad's knee at every given opportunity. Thus it was a learning curve for him too.

Though we had a four-bed roomed house space was at a premium. After sharing a double bedroom, with a double bed and bunk beds therein, I had to move into a small bedroom with Paula in a cot at the side. Terry had the smallest bedroom on his own. Janice, Marie, Ella and Lynn were in the big double.

Paula was a nightmare. She used to wake early on a morning and start banging her cot – this entailed standing up holding onto a side and rocking back and forth – noisily. She did this so much that she broke the sprung base and Dad had to fix it. Then she too practiced escapism. She would climb out over the bars. She got out once and liberally clarted up my dressing table with some 'nice gooey' stuff she found in a tube – my make-up. I don't know what is in make-up but it would not come off after it had dried. Dad made a string mesh cover that he fixed all round the top of the cot to prevent her escape. When she was very young I used to change and feed her in the night sometimes to give Mum a break. As Paula came to live with us for a few years in later life I suppose I became a sort of surrogate Mum allowing for our age difference. Paula and my daughter are certainly more like sisters than aunt and niece.

Dad sounds pretty handy but we were still the cobbler's kids including Mum. She had an old gate style clothes airer which had the audacity to have a broken piece. She asked him if he could get one of the joiners to mend it. After 15 years she threw it out – still broken. To give him his due he did build things for us. He built Terry's peddle car out of scrap bits and he built various bikes for us over the years. Spanner was a very practical Dad.

The Dalestars and Other Musical Forays

Dad played the trumpet, and didn't we know it. Every night without fail he would practice in his office which, by the strategically predestined design of the building, fell directly below my bedroom. So, if I wanted to escape the noise and general fracas that a house full of children embraced I had to do it to the accompaniment of 'When the Saints Go Marching in.' He did alternate this with obscure tunes intermittently punctuated with the odd out-of-tune notes, but invariably it would be a stop-start background torture. Peace transcended when he decided it was time to go for a drink and play his interminable darts. Naturally he was the darts captain, and for many years at the Kings Arms in the High Street. Over the years he could readily boast of having been darts captain at many watering holes in the dale.

Musically he was quite accomplished in that he played many instruments by now. Through this interest he got together with other likeminded dales men and in 1958 they formed a small dance band which was similar to a skiffle group but without the washboard. They did however have someone playing a tea chest. This was a box with a pole and strung at an angle from the top to the chest. This was plucked to accommodate a double base sound and it worked.

They played in many village halls including Greenhow, Darley and Embsay and in the local pubs. They played in the dining room of the Talbot, which is now a guest house. This dining room was upstairs but it did have the modern convenience of a dumb waiter and this was used to get their instruments upstairs. I distinctly remember them playing at the Drill Hall in Bridgehousegate which I was allowed to attend though I am not sure why. I do remember thinking it was quite amusing to be doing this in what was ostensibly our school dinner room. The teachers at Bridgehousegate Primary School used to regimentally march all us children across the main road, up a small road and along two ginnels to reach the Drill Hall. My other memories of the room were of that foul smell of boiled cabbage and insalubrious school gravy with a definite hint of 'this is not going to taste very nice' that hit you when you walked in. And here we were dancing away in that very room. Cool.

Len blowing his own trumpet and John tickling his ivories

Brian did well and was offered a good job working for Leeds City Varieties so they had to get another drummer and Tom Jagger took over. Tom in turn got his uncle, Harry Harrison, interested and he joined the band playing the violin. This broadened their repertoire slightly and their geographical practice venues. They used to go all the way to Harry's house in Huby to practice on some occasions. Such dedication.

Harry Harrison on violin, Dad on trumpet, John Breckon on piano,
don't know who is on lightshade and Tom Jagger is on drums –
what a team

They practiced up at Scar and even practiced at 'Kingsclere' on occasions.

Barbara, John's wife, particularly remembers playing cards at 'Kingsclere' and the laughter. There was a core of about six couples that used to do this and sometimes the venue would be at one of the other player's houses. They drank within reason, laughed a lot and smoked a lot and I seem to recall that they played for mere coppers. (pennies and 'apennies)

Apparently they used to buy music – orchestral scores with parts for the piano, drums etc. John said that when he put some music in front of Ted Timlin once he said *"blimey who's thrown damp teapot dregs over this, it looks like all t'tea leaves are all over it!"* They managed however and played often by ear and got regular work. Tunes John recalls are 'Whispering', 'Lady Be Good' and a Sidney Thompson arrangement for barn dance – a medley of different tunes.

On one occasion they had been practicing at Huby and they, along with their equipment, were all in Dad's big black car – one he used for funerals of course. Mum phoned Dad at Huby to tell him that a funeral had come in; someone at Bishop Thornton had passed away. Well Dad did not want to trail all the way back to Pateley and then have to go back in the same direction so obviously he treated them to a detour. He took them all with him to visit the deceased. They were all invited inside and Barbara remembers they all sat round an old fire range and an elderly lady gave them a drink while Dad went upstairs to do the 'measuring up'. What a trouper. He went back the following day to collect the body. From thereon practice nights took on a whole new meaning.

They never really split up they just drifted apart. John started on his own playing in pubs. He bought an organ which was a darned sight easier to sing along to as it held a variety of background beats. He often played at The Conservative Club and at The Crown. He says *"there were allus some good singers; I remember Stan Light, Granville Chadwick and Joe Derrick. We 'ad some right good sing songs in there"*

They did however tend to change the words of some songs to be slightly more risqué and with words like these audience participation was a 'slam dunk'

John progressed onto bigger things and got some weekend resident work at a club in Ripon then High Harrogate (Arrigut) Working Men's Club approached him to play there at weekends. More money, no contest. Then he was offered a mid-week dance slot with the room for free and to keep all the entrance charges while they got the benefit of increased bar takings. By this time he was forming his own dance band – The Hammond Sound. They played all over Yorkshire with jobs as far afield as Scotch Corner, and many in Leeds and Harrogate (Arrigut). They used to support all the big bands including The Millermen. They never had a problem involving the audience as it was popular stuff they were playing and singing along was a prerequisite enjoyed by all. They even sang some slightly risqué wording to 'Bye Bye Blackbird' which always went down a treat; they sang it the correct way in the first section then with the new invigorated wording in the second section, but it is best left unwritten for the purpose of this book! It did however have its embarrassing side in that the audience tended to be more active when The Hammonds were on than when the main band came on.

Dad too did not stop playing his music either though not in the same way as John. He went on to play the cornet with Lofthouse and Middlesmoor Brass Band with whom he played for over twenty years.

In later years he got pleasure from playing electric organs of which he had several. We were often treated to a rendition whenever we visited him. Luckily his musical talents had increased immensely from those early years.

He always managed to produce a tune from his beloved mouth organ.

Lofthouse & Middlesmoor Brass Band

The wonderful Lofthouse and Middlesmoor Brass Band was formed even before the First World War and has survived both wars heroically. A meeting at Lofthouse Crown Hotel resulted in the first bandmaster, the pub licensee, being appointed and he was paid the princely sum of a £1 annual salary. They managed to purloin music from another dales band and bought some new instruments along with some second-hand horns and bases. And so another dales institution was born. Initially there was a lot of interest and those who wanted to join the band were subject to selection followed by a 3 month trial. This was strictly adhered to and those who did not attend regularly would be suspended.

As the band gained notoriety they were invited to play at the Middlesmoor Bell Festival in 1915. From then on very many bookings came in and they played at concerts all over the dale. They were an established entity of great appreciation. Amazingly of all those from the band who were called up in the First World World war only one was wounded and they all came back. By 1919 in was decided that they would have uniforms costing a huge £3.15s.0d which they individually paid for in instalments. Progression yet again and it was decided to have their instruments silver-plated to give each musician pride in their band and thus they became a silver band. After winning the Muker Band Contest at Swaledale they attained the new status of being a prize silver band and became known from thereon as Lofthouse and Middlesmoor Prize Silver Band – quite a mouthful.

At the onset of the Second World War again there was a shortage of musicians as many had 'gone to war' and outsiders had to be drafted in to make up their numbers. Time of course marches on even for a Silver/ Brass Band and it had been noticed that membership was dwindling. In the 60's it was decided to actually embrace the fact that there are two sexes on this planet and women were invited to join so it was no longer a 'men only' band. Today the band has an equal number of male and female musicians.

Gladys Blakeson was one of these and is a stalwart of the band as she started back in 1961, paying two shillings and sixpence for the privilege, and is still blowing her trumpet – tenor horn to be precise. But she has every right to blow her trumpet so to speak. She started on the cornet but couldn't quite hit the high notes so the bandmaster suggested the tenor horn and she's been doing it ever since. After her first husband passed away she met her second husband in the band – he played the euphonium. Now that is romantic – nowadays romance embraces texting, e mail, facebook and tweeting or some such thing – not quite the same.

The annual Middlesmoor Bell Festival parade. Dad is on the back row and the only one without an instrument to his lips.

Dad played with the band all over the dales throughout the years. The men who worked for him loved it when he went off to play at shows as it meant a bit of an easy going day. They played at many shows including Kilnsey Show and as support to the main brass band at Nidderdale Show. They did an annual stint at Tanhill – the highest pub in England. This was another 'all day' job and they had a huge amount of fun doing it. They would stop for lunch 'going up' and have a good time accompanied by a drink thereafter.

They played every Christmas, much to Mum's disgust, as it meant Dad 'got away' much of Christmas Day AND Boxing Day leaving her to cope with a houseful of rowdy, excited, 'Christmas presented up' and sometimes 'chucking up' kids (Yorkshire for children) on her own.

So that was Mum's Christmas; Dad's was playing in the villages – Lofthouse and Middlesmoor on Christmas day and lower down the dale to Ramsgill on Boxing Day – along with stopping at various farms and trundling up their lanes with their instruments to play and be 'meted and greeted' with copious amounts of alcohol, Christmas cake, mince pies and pork pie.

Who got most chilled at Christmas, Mum or Dad – no contest.

On one occasion they had some instruments in a van going to a farm and the back door flew open sending a drum tumbling right down the hill. It is not known whether this poor unfortunate survived the ordeal.

Gladys remembered one Christmas in the village at Lofthouse, Harry the bass player always came early in the morning visiting locals as he only lived a mile away. Thus by the time they got started at 10.30 am he had 'ad a few drinks'. They led up to the top of the village to the fountain in the middle and were playing away when suddenly Harry keeled over flat on his back with his big bass still strapped to him. 'That were the end of 'arry for the day'.

They even played on other nights at Christmas covering some farms up to Scar. Nowadays they play slightly less often only playing on Boxing Day; however they do play in the High Street on Christmas shopping evenings.

Terry also started to play the cornet, and joined the band as a boy, in the fervent hope he could do the bonding thing with Dad. Initially it appeared to be doing the trick, but it soon lost its attraction as Terry tended to get 'shoved into a corner' as he put it under those old auspices of 'children should be seen and not heard' that still prevailed. He got fed up in the end and left Dad to it. Ella followed in later years and of all of us was the most musically inclined and was able to read music well, which is quite frankly Latin to me. I did try to learn the trumpet and managed to issue forth with one scale and that is where I finished. Dad as a tutor and me as a pupil did not gel. Patience had not been issued in either of our curriculums of character traits.

A band dinner. These were smashing Do's.

From the left running clockwise is Sidney Alderson, Our Terry, John Breckon, Dad, Bobby Lee, Lena Lee, Gwen Allen, Norman Lee, Dinah Lee, Joe Firth, Wilf Watson and Betty Wilson (hopefully those names are right!)

Terry Recalls......

Terry has very scant memories of Dacre as he was only four when we moved to Pateley. He remembers his Uncle Jack, Jack Geldart who lived next door, who used to sit him on his knee. He also remembers pushing me down the hole in the yard with his pedal car and even after all this time is asserting that he did not do it on purpose. Well of course I believe him, not.

He does specifically remember when he and I were sent to stay with Aunt Irene, mum's sister, down in Calcot for three months one summer. Mum was having a pregnancy health problem at the time. I know I thoroughly enjoyed staying there and I had my cousin Hazel to play with.

Terry however was a different kettle of fish. We both spoke good old Yorkshire; the accent didn't bother me much purely because I pick up dialects easily and was soon speaking southern. Terry however was dyed in the wool Yorkshire. This was his first experience of school and, because of his strange accent he got rather bullied by a young lad from a local estate. He took the punishment a little to start with but soon fought back and the parent of this child came round to see Aunt Irene to complain about this 'Yorkshire Bully'. The complaint was totally untrue and the fact that Terry had fought back gave him 'street cred' as the bully was not very well liked. Henceforth the class all proceeded to learn Yorkshire and he left a class full of kids speaking it.

He too said he had a good childhood and I am thoroughly convinced that the yard played a huge part in this. He didn't watch much television and spent as much time outside as he could playing with his friends and getting up to good old ubiquitous mischief. He suspected some of the men did not like him too much as he was always up to something and a bit of a pest. When he found they had put his toy bulldozer in the cement mixer it was a bit of a dead giveaway!

He said that he always felt a bit sad when he thought of Dad because he was always searching for that bonding thing that just seemed to evade them. Dad did build things for him though even though they did not spend much time together but it was the latter that Terry would have liked.

Dad built him a pedal car that Terry recalled as being 'the most beautiful thing' with blow up tyres and spoked wheels. This eventually got chopped up and he took the wheels and steering off and put them on a bogey. Like father like son.

Terry's friends were Dave Gamble, and Wilf and Jack Holdsworth at the time and they used to race their bogeys all over, with no brakes or helmets of course.

In the 60's when he started secondary school the children used to do metalwork using a lathe so Dad bought Terry a lathe for Christmas which cost him £30. But that's as far as it went. The lathe stayed under Terry's bed for nearly six months and in the end he got it out on his own and set it up. Then he got a rollicking for setting it up wrong. Terry didn't understand why he had spent so much money on this lathe and then not helped him set it up. He couldn't win; he tried very hard to please him but never seemed to achieve it. It was such a shame. As Terry got older Dad seemed to expect even more of him which made their relationship somewhat strained.

Terry today accepts that this was what Dad was all about. He worked very hard, and he provided for us well and in his own way he cared. Terry, like the rest of us, believed it was Mum that held the family together.

Trips and holidays were all instigated by Mum. If she had not paid the deposit for going to Butlins each time then we would never have gone. She told him later and naturally Dad didn't want to waste the deposit. She knew 'im well.

Homeward journey from trip to seaside – note the removable seats you don't get that sort of adaptability in vehicles these days

Terry started driving virtually as soon as he could reach the pedals. As Little King Street (aka the lane) is an unmade road, he had his playground for this. Dad had an old black standard Atlas van which Terry decided to drive down the lane. He had Jack Holdsworth in the front with a couple of lads in the back. He drove it flat out and got up to 30 mph as he got to the yard. He had to brake so hard his foot went straight through the floor. They travelled into the yard and into the shed and slid to a stop just a hairs breadth away from the wagon parked in front. They were well shaken up. That was the first of Terry's nine lives.

The first job he remembered being involved with was at Summerstone Lodge on the road up to Scar reservoir. This was in 1963 ish and he would only be around twelve years old. Dad paid him 3d (three old pence) per hour. He loved going up to Summerstone because it gave him the opportunity to drive as there was a corporation road there. He took a huge liking to it but his driving skills were the source of much concern in later years. He remembered quite a bit about this job and said

"Old Billy wasn't too nice to me but his son 'Wiggy' was very good to me, I loved working with Wiggy"

The church at Thruscross brought forth a splattering of expletives from Terry *"what a stupid building that were for a church, it 'ad an inverted roof"* Terry would have been about fourteen at the time and driving an old jalopy whenever he could sneak it. He used to load up with materials from the bottom and bring them up to the site. He passed his test at sixteen. He got to drive the JCB, before he was old enough, He said *"there were a load of muck wanted shifting and the men said they'd shift it first thing Monday morning. I got there about 'alf past three and said blow it can do it before five o'clock and jumped in the JCB. Three quarters of an hour later it were on its side in the road. One of 'em said he were not surprised as when I turned the JCB the back wheels left the floor"* This was the second of his nine lives.

There would have been hell to pay from Dad, which is doubtless why Terry is now rolling about with laughter.

"on the same job I was old enough to drive the JCB by now and I were coming down the side of the reservoir flat out in top gear. I couldn't see because the weight of it 'ad forced it over on its governors and there were black smoke coming out" This was the third of his nine lives.

Terry is still rolling about with laughter.

He was once driving the JCB down Lupton Bank, near Glasshouses, and it jumped out of gear. Then *"I stalled the engine and I were going down Lupton Bank wi' no power steering or anything. I nearly poo'd mi pants that day"* This was the fourth of his nine lives.

Terry is still rolling about with laughter.

How Terry is still here to be able to roll about with laughter is a total mystery.

He used to be quite creative in attempts to carry out some jobs that required an innovative method to carry them out, or in other words a 'Heath Robinson' approach. One such was the painting of Nidd Church clock. They had a sixteen foot extension ladder but it was about fifty to sixty feet up. He said *"So I went up the tower and slung a rope down pulling part of this ladder up and tied it to the top of the tower. Then I pulled the other 'alf of the ladder up and tied that. I got some ladder brackets and some scaffolding posts. Then I went down the ladder from the top and painted the clock. It worked, where there's a will there's a way. Lord Mount Garrett came along and said 'oh that's 'ow you do it'. I think 'e thought it were a regular occurrence to do these sorts of jobs!"*

Bravado was always part of Terry's vocabulary. That teenage 'no fear' phase lasted him well into his twenties. *"I were well stupid when I were young'* he said.

'I've been a bit if a mischief in mi time and set folks up. Pete Shearstone, bless 'im, were a young lad and he were frightened of 'eights. We were working on a roof which 'ad a double apex with a valley in over a parapet and there were a little string course that stuck out about six inches. I climbed onto the parapet and were clinging on and shouting to Pete to come and 'elp me. 'e forced 'imself to come down that roof to get me and just as 'e got there and stood up – I were on the little string ledge. He were well upset and I said don't worry Pete. He wouldn't forgive me for that one. So easy to go at stuff without thinking"

Dad had a cremation come in and he was not averse to keeping Terry off school to help. *"Dad nicked me off school to help. If I wasn't needed I would sit in the 'earse between the driver and Dad. Thus I became the 'third passenger' which normally referred to the person in the back. On this occasion the cremation were in Arrigut* (Harrogate). *The cortege 'ad got reversed for the homeward journey. We set off back in this old 'earse, that belonged to another Dales company and driven by one of their drivers, with relatives cars in front. The 'earse were about fifty'horse power with big sweeping wings and big lamps and the whole thing used to flap about. We ran over a manhole and it must 'ave affected something because the speed said something like forty miles an 'our and I started laughing. Dad asked me what I were laughing at and I said well that speedo says it will do 140 miles an 'our and I reckon if we go any faster than this the wings 'ud fall off. This upset the driver and 'e took great exception to it and after we got through Burnt Yates 'e put 'is foot down. 'e shot forward and passed the funeral cortege and got it up to ninety miles an 'our before he got to the bend at the bottom. Don't know what those poor folk thought at this funeral. A Rolls Royce 'earse doing 90 miles an hour"*

Other funeral jobs Terry undertook were digging graves. He had one to dig at Hartwith Church and he was not very popular for that one. He did not dig it big enough and the coffin, that was bigger than normal, would not go down. He had to go and dig out more but he only did the length and forgot about the width and the coffin still would not go down. *"Dad were well pleased"*

He had to dig one at Dacre Church. The vicar set out where the grave should be dug but they were very closely spaced. *"it were a bit close and I were digging away and I went through the corner of the grave next door. It were a Sunday about dusk and all were quiet and I though I'll just 'ave a peak. I got mi matches and struck one and put it up to this little hole and something inside went puff and blew it out, so I thought. I were like Popeye, I jumped up in t'air and ran like billio from that grave. I know now that it were just lack of air that made the match go out but it were well scary"*

Something similar happened up at the small graveyard at Greenhow. This graveyard stands alone directly by the roadside. Again it was dusk and miserable and damp. Two of the men were digging a grave and one went off to the Miner's pub (no longer exists) to get refreshments, leaving one down the hole. He apparently put his spade in at one point and there was this awful liquid sucking noise. He jumped out of that grave and refused point blank to go back.

When Terry was about seventeen they were doing a job relating to changing to natural gas and they had a base to put in for a gasometer. There were quite high penalty clauses if the job was not finished on time so there were quite high bonuses for completing on time. Terry was working with Jonty Middleton as his apprentice and they agreed they would share the bonus. *"we needed two loads of 'ardcore to finish off, but Dad told me I could only get one so off I went up to Greenhow quarry. I got 'em to load up and there were only half inch clearance between the body and the wheels. I went over the weighbridge with seven and a half tons on the back. Coming down Greenhow the vehicle jumped out of gear and I 'ad all on to control it. I said 'one load Dad but you didn't say how much I could put on it' – I don't think he were too amused but we did get the job finished on time. I got a huge £175 from that"*

Terry and Dad continued to have these father and son spats peculiar to most fathers and sons. Theirs were quite difficult because each wanted something from the other that neither could give.

He thought the world of Mum as did we all. He thought she was clever and he could not remember her ever telling him off. *"but you always knew when you 'ad upset 'er and knew when to back off. I 'ad a lot of respect for Mum. By the time I were sixteen Dad and me used to curse each other like there were no tomorrow"*

When they finally did fall out Terry went to work at St. James Grammar School on full money at eighteen. He didn't like the work but he was earning good money.

As for being a boy amongst many girls it never really bothered him as he mainly did his own thing. We all had ups and downs with each other as is normal in most families but Terry's lot as a child was a happy one despite not getting Dad feedback.

The years passed with Dad and Terry not on speaking terms for quite some time. It is only since he has lived down in Cambridge that the atmosphere eased and they got back on speaking terms, which is good because even though Dad was never demonstrative he cared greatly for his only son.

Last Train from Pateley

It was decided by powers that be that the train line from Harrogate to Pateley Bridge would have to close as it was not making money. In April 1961 the last train from Pateley left the station. It was a sad day for the dale and to mark the occasion local schoolchildren were to be the last passengers.

As Marie was in the top class at the infant's school she was to be on this train. The teachers took them, crocodile fashion, to the railway station and Marie was concerned they were running a bit late. When they got to the station Mrs Morris realised they had forgotten the straws for the' ever present school milk' and promptly asked Marie to run back for them. She was aghast and was convinced she was going to miss the train. She ran like back like billio (Yorkshire for like the wind) constantly thinking we're late, we're late – a bit like in Alice in Wonderland. She was convinced they would not hold the train up for her and was on panic mode. She pulled the cupboard open spilling all the contents, grabbed the straws and ran back with tears streaming down her face. When she got there she saw Mrs Morris had held the train up for her. Marie is well proud she was the last person to get on the last train from Pateley.

It was shown on the news on the television that night and all you saw was a teacher dragging a child with glasses along the platform – Marie. Mum and Dad let her stay up and watch it again later. Everyone has to be famous for something!

The railway workmen used to give rides to the local children on the platelayer's pump trolley and take them along the line as far as Glasshouses. Marie was not that suited though because the younger children could only go as far as Harefield then had to get off. She was one of the younger children and most chagrined that she could not stay on all the way to Glasshouses.

Pateley Bridge Railway Station – lines of communication

Schoolchildren waiting to board Last Train from Pateley

Pictures courtesy of Nidderdale Museum

Butlins

Butlins holidays were absolutely brilliant. The whole family, except Dad, were overjoyed when holiday time came round. Dad used to take the family and stay just one night and go back home. He would then do a repeat run on the Friday night staying another night and take us home on the Saturday.

We went to Butlins every year for a few years. It was always with eager anticipation we set off on holiday and it never failed to surprise us every time we went. There was something new each year. The children's playground was just swings and roundabouts in the early years with a big wheel and then a merry go round, a small switch back and a whip roundabout were added. The best bit was that it did not cost anything to go on the rides and when you got off them you could join the queue to go on again. Sheer bliss for children. The main camp changed every year with bigger and better bars and shopping. Who can forget the Beachcomber bar with the sound effects at one end and scene change from day to night? It was such a novelty to be able to go to the bar and buy a Tom Collins with straw and umbrella. There was the boating lake which was very pretty and well laid out with foliage and a small train that ran all around the perimeter. Ducks had taken up residence. There was even a boxing ring with wrestling matches staged which Dad enjoyed. The rope railway which ran to the shore, was a five to ten minute walk away, gave spectacular views of Filey bay and of course the holiday camp.

Whilst on holiday Sam Firth, speaker of the broadest of Yorkshire accents, visited us there and was persuaded to go to the beach. He could not however be persuaded to go on the rope railway. Mum was in one of the chairs about half way along when it stopped suddenly and Mum was left dangling for a while. Sam, shouted at the top of his voice "*I teld thee thee buggers it wont safe*" and he was laughing 'fit to kill' Mum often told this tale but she was cringing at the time.

There were various styles of chalet, some with a porch front. The chalets were denoted in alphabetical order then numbered and this extended to well over a hundred to each row. They were expanded over the years and outer ones gained a second floor along with self-catering being introduced.

The one thing I looked forward to mostly was the programme and pouring over it when we arrived to mark out all the best things to go and see and do. We did not want to miss anything and if anything was a close call we would race to the next event. We even loved the 'Wakey Wakey' call on a morning preceded by a 'ding dong' sound.

There were two huge dining rooms, one at each end of the camp. There were two sittings and each sitting had a house name which you were assigned to, and acceded to being a member of, for competitions for the whole week. I remember the names Kent and Gloucester and there were others. The food was very good with a full cooked breakfast, and three course dinner. It was very noisy. Every day the Red Coats would 'spin the clock' – this was to spin for a table number and then a row number. The winning table was awarded the spectacle of a crocodile of Red Coats parading to their table with an ice bucket with champagne all to the accompaniment of the whole room clapping on the beat of the march. It was brilliant. Each year we hoped we might win it but the dining room was vast with a lot of people hoping for the same thing.

One particular week we were away I decided to enter the Holiday Princess competition. I was a nervous wreck parading about in front of all those people. Furthermore the judging panel actually had the camp vicar as one of the judges. I won, much to Mum's glee when I told her. The presentation was to be on the Friday so Mum insisted I wear a dress I did not much like as I thought it a bit young, but one does as one's mother says. I was not too pleased however as I got a cup and I would rather have got the second place for a big box of Max Factor goodies. Immediately after the presentation we had to go to the dining room for tea – this was when our previous hopes actually came true, we won the champagne spin. It was pretty good to finally win but not so good to have to stand on a chair in front of all those people drinking from this silver trophy cup I had been presented with. Embarrassing or what. Well I was just seventeen and that is grown up – or so I thought.

Various competitions were held throughout the week and house points awarded accordingly. Everybody entered into the spirit of things and competitiveness was embraced with fervour.

Mum could relax and feel safe that all of us children were ok even though we went off and did our own thing. We just loved being able to do our own thing.

We were all very sad when Butlins closed. The memories of swimming in the indoor pool, the cacophony of noise and the smell of the chlorine remain. I can still hear and smell it now if I close my eyes and daydream. Swimming by the side windows that lined the walls of the pool where people could see you swimming was brilliant. The Viennese ballroom was also quite wonderful. Columns were camouflaged as tree trunks and there were overhanging walkways disguised as houses and we ran all over. Pure magic.

It is hard to comprehend the previous usage of Butlins. As children we were in that place we all value so much particularly as we get entrenched in adulthood. Those were the days of exciting discoveries and new learnings about everything and anything, about new relationships with none of the encumbrances that adulthood bestows on us. That our wonderful Butlins had been the venue for the previous procurement was hard to accept. To later learn that Dad had been stationed in Filey, adjacent to Butlins, during the war that shaped our futures was also quite dampening. The two usages of Butlins just did not go together and almost sullied our wonderful memories. Places are just places to be occupied in time in accordance therewith, but to children places can be absolutely magical.

Here's proof that Dad stay with us for a little while before hightailing it back to 'Kingsclere' to look after work.

Ella, Terry, Me and Jan at one of those oh so happy and noisy mealtimes

Fun between the chalet lines in 1961 Marie, friend Denise,
Terry and Me

Jan and Terry learning to swim in indoor pool

The Watson posse photo-shoot

Many families holidaying at Butlins had a group photograph at one time
or another. This was ours taken around 1965/66.

Left to right – Ella, Jan, Dad, Terry, Lynn, Mum, Me and Marie
– only one more to go to complete the whole brood.

Time Travel Onwards Relentlessly

The eleven plus was a part of school life that we all had to expect. I took mine at Bridgehousegate School and passed. However there were many passes that year and not enough places and, as mine was a lower mark, I was told I could hope for a place during the following year or I could take a thirteen plus, but they only did these every two years. I finished up taking a thirteen plus when I was twelve and eventually went to Harrogate Grammar School. What a palaver. Whilst waiting to take my thirteen plus Mum and Dad decided to take me out of mainstream and sent me to a Carradyls – girl's private school in the hills above Pateley. The main reason they sent me there was that Dad had done some work for the school and they owed him some money and it would be their way of paying the bill. Dale's folk were good at that.

This put me between a rock and a hard place. The local children thought I was posh and thus too stuck up to talk to and the girls at school thought I was common because I spoke Yorkshire and was not posh. So I became somewhat lonely and I resented the way the girls at school treated me. This was however about to change. There were a couple of incidents at the school that finally got me accepted and I began to enjoy being there. I know I felt I learned more in those few terms than in the years I spent at the Grammar school. Mum used to laugh at me because she said I spoke posh when I was in the grounds of the school but the moment I got out of the gates I was almost back to being Yorkshire. However sending me to Carradyls was a parental gesture that they could not continue as it was costly and private education for all of us was out of the question. Jan went to St Peters Girls School in Harrogate and thereafter Terry and Marie went to Pateley School. Ella went to

Harrogate Grammar School and Paula finished up going to Rossett Green in Harrogate.

Going to school in Harrogate meant being up early so I often had breakfast with Dad before catching the bus. Sometimes I missed it and had to take the famous No. 24 which I had to pay for and arrive late. At seventeen I could not wait to leave school. I had been a 'Saturday girl' at Woolworths to earn some money and the manager asked me if I would like a full time job as shrinkage assistant doing office work. I wanted to but I was not flavour of the month with Mum and Dad. Dad was disgusted that I was going to work at Woolworths. Anyway I got my way and enjoyed working there. When I decided to leave the manager wanted to make me up to shrinkage supervisor but I had run the gauntlet with Woolworths by then. I was to go to the Careers office, as they called it, but was too scared to go in. Trying to think up an excuse for not going in I thought I'd say 'wouldn't it be a good idea to work for Dad'. What was I thinking!

Thus I started working for Dad in the office. I did all the typing of letters, invoices and I did the wages, for a pittance I would add. However I did get to learn to drive as he thought it would be a good idea if I could take the men to work on sites. I did not do this much though after taking Mum's car, loaded with men, and scraping all down the side of it getting too close to a wall.

I went through all the old sales invoices and found very many that were old and had not been paid. I promptly started writing to the debtors in no uncertain terms. One man in particular came to see Dad and said *'I thought we were friends Len'* – his bill was over five years old! He obviously thought Dad should have worked for free. A little of that attitude was certainly prevalent in some of the older Dales folk. Bartering had long since declined but bills remained unpaid in the forlorn hope that they might somehow cease to be credible.

When I worked for Dad Lynn was about four years old and I saw a lot of her. When she started school I remember standing with Mum at the front door watching her go skipping down the lane to school and feeling very sad. She used to rush into the office when she came home with the latest artistic effort for my approval. She was a little tinker though.

The office was a bit shabby and Dad would not let me have any wallpaper so I cut up an old wallpaper samples book and papered one wall. Then I asked for paint and all he would let me have was some pale blue gloss paint. So I painted the makeshift desk (two chests of drawers with a dropped bit between with the Remington typewriter on) this lovely shade of pale blue. Yuck. I also painted the safe that was on the floor in the corner and in black paint I picked out the letters around the key hole which looked quite smart. Then the safe keys went missing so Dad had to blow it open. Eventually the keys were found in Lynn's little handbag at the back of the toy cupboard. Did I say she was a little tinker?

Double Wedding Day

In 1968 my fiancée Tony and I wanted to get married, however so did Janis and her boyfriend Pete. We were subsequently told that unfortunately two weddings could not be afforded so we had a double wedding.

On 23rd March 1968 I married Tony and Janis married Pete. The wedding reception was held at Foster Beck. This is a large building about a mile or so above Pateley and has a huge water wheel which is today a working water wheel. It is a lovely building which has lent itself to being a public house and subject to many changes over the years. It also entertained many rock gigs and folk concerts. It is currently a hotel and the license has moved to a building nearby. Naturally of course the reason for having the reception there was because the then owner owed Dad some money for work done and this was a way to pay it back.

Paula stole the day though. When all were dutifully seated at the long tables arranged as a big 'U' shape, Paula in her inimitable manner, walked along the front of the head table proudly pronouncing that she wanted a wee wee.

It was a lovely day with lots of guests and all Mums siblings made it for the occasion. It was only marred by one thing. Our Lynn was not there.

In those days – and I keep trying to avoid this phrase as it is time worn but necessary, it was customary for the bride and groom to leave after the reception so they missed out on all the frivolity. Tony and I arranged to leave in style. We borrowed my brother's bubble car. It was quite a sight tearing away at the break neck speed of about twenty miles an hour with the usual array of adornments guaranteed to embarrass.

We made our way to our new abode in Harrogate. No 12, Olive Grove was our very first house where we spent the next seven years.

Jan and Pete were going up to the Knott – a house above Pateley that Dad was in the process of renovating.

Arrival at St Cuthbert's Church on a windy day in March
Terry, Jan, Dad, Gill and Colin (Pete's brother)

Little Lynn

Then came one of the saddest times of our lives.

There was a 'bug' that was doing the rounds in Pateley and little Lynn got it. She was sick and did not seem to be getting better. Mum called the doctor who immediately called an ambulance for her. I remember picking little Paula up so she could see Lynn through the back window of the ambulance when they took her away.

All this happened just four weeks before Jan and I were due to have our double wedding.

When she went into Harrogate General hospital the Children's specialist told us that Lynn's kidneys had collapsed. He told us she had a kidney problem that was very rare and it was as a result of the 'bug' that had been going round. He tried to explain it to us by saying that as one child could eat strawberries and be alright another would get a rash. This is how the 'bug' had affected Lynn. One of the nurses had tried to look up the problem and it was not even recorded in the hospital library.

Lynn was in a room on her own. All of us visited her when we could. Mum went during the day and Dad went early evening. As I lived in Harrogate after the wedding I could go regularly and often went on my lunch break from work to sit with her.

We still had Lynn's bridesmaid dress made but she never got to wear it.

Some weeks after the wedding Tony and I called into the hospital before going out with friends. Mum met us in the corridor and told us she had been given forty eight hours. Now I am crying. Even after all these years.

When I next visited her it was so very hard. She said to me *"Gill I am not going to come out of hospital am I?"* I cringed inside and mustered what little I had left and more or less said that the doctor had said that she might be let out on Saturday if she kept on doing well. I remember I mentioned Saturday as it was only the beginning of the week when she asked me this and at least she would still think she would be coming home right until the end. That was so hard.

Lynn kept on going right up until Saturday and then we lost her.

She was five years old. She died in Dad's arms.

Dad came down to our house and we knew before he got to the door. There are no words.

It was just four weeks after Jan and I had got married thus the family house was reduced by three offspring in a matter of weeks.

At her funeral in St. Cuthbert's Church we sang Lynn's favourite hymn 'All Things Bright and Beautiful' and I remember looking up at the stained glass window. I know I was trying to mouth the words but no sound was coming out.

Afterwards Mum struggled to accept what had happened.

There were two things that happened not long after Lynn went that were very disquieting and hard to believe. Mum received a letter from some would be 'do gooder' organisation trying to explain that it was God's will and he had a garden and he could pick the flowers. Oh dear. The other discomfiting occurrence was when Mum was in the High Street and a local person, thankfully I do not know who, shouted across the road asking Mum if she had got over the death of her child and not to worry because she had other children. Such gross insensitivity.

Losing Lynn was an awful time in our lives and affected us all very badly. Janis and I obviously no longer lived at 'Kingsclere' and just over a year later Terry got married. It meant seven children at home had depleted to just three in a very short space of time.

Even now I believe we all miss little Lynn. I recently did the 'visit a spiritualist' trip, nursing a definite cynical attitude. The lady told me of a child flitting about. Naturally of course it all pointed to Lynn. She said she was mischievous and tended to hide things. She said if a picture was askew at home or if I lost things then it was this child being mischievous. I left that venue and lost my keys in the process. I went back, not exactly thinking I would find them but lo and behold they had been handed in. Now of course whenever we lose anything we automatically think our Lynn is up to mischief. It keeps her alive in our hearts.

Mum

Mum had not been enjoying the best of health for some time. She had always been a heavy smoker and indeed all of us followed suit only to give up in later years.

Over the coming years she developed angina and arterial sclerosis which affected her walking. She slowly became unable to walk very far and began to suffer excruciating pain. This eventually got so bad that she had to be hospitalised. She had developed a large ulcer on her leg and was ultimately sent to St James Hospital in Leeds with a view to having her leg amputated but the surgeon decided instead to remove the ulcer. Mum was in agony and begging them to remove her leg as they had originally intended. I visited her and she was extremely distraught as it transpired that apparently the ward doctor had indicated that he could not understand why the surgeon had done what he had and not amputated. I spoke with the sister and hit the roof over this. The surgeon amputated her leg shortly afterwards.

The pain subsided but now Mum was left with the problems of healing and of phantom pains in the leg that was no longer there. The amputation wound did not initially heal and she had to have a further operation. I thus insisted that she came to stay with me so that I could look after her until the stump started to get better, much to Dad's chagrin as he still expected Mum to do any office work that needed doing.

Luckily this was a success and Mum came to terms with her new status. They originally gave her a prosthetic metal thing with a club stump on the end of it which was unnerving for children to see. Her subsequent leg, which took some time to make, was certainly an improvement on that but nowhere near as good as the limbs that are made today.

Mum was awarded a mobility car, a little blue mini, and she got a new lease of life travelling all over. Seaside trips were regular.

Things were starting to look up.

No they weren't.

Mums poor circulation did not help and of course she still smoked. She went on to develop a stomach ulcer. She received long treatment for this but eventually suffered a perforated ulcer. Sickness became a way of life.

She started to lose a lot of weight and it took the medical profession the better part of a year to discover she had an overactive thyroid gland. She was put on medication for this and started to improve. Then she started having headaches and she was blithely told that the tablets she was on could not be causing the headaches and it was not investigated further.

In July 1976 she was rushed into hospital yet again. Poor Marie and Paula were on their own when Mum became very ill. Marie sent Paula out looking for Dad and she rang me and said the doctor would not come. I hit the roof but could not do much from Harrogate. Marie had coped very well under the circumstances. While looking for Dad Paula had spoken to a friend, Margaret Hill from the Royal Oak, and she came over and rang the doctor. Marie said Margaret played holy war with the doctor and swore at him on the phone. An ambulance was called. This time Mum had a brain tumour.

I rushed to the hospital and as I lived in Harrogate I got there first. I was livid and gave vent to my fury with one of the doctors in the hospital. He could not unfortunately give me any good news. My friend Shilly was with us at the time and she tried to calm me down. Mum was by this time unconscious.

A day or so later I got a phone call from the hospital asking me to go. I rang Pateley, left my baby Richard with a neighbour and charged to the hospital.

I was too late.

Our Mum, my mentor, my best friend, my everything had gone. I was inconsolable.

I asked if I could sit with Mum until the family arrived and the nurses let me. I spoke to Mum and it was a very special and precious time for me.

Dad arrived in the hospital and Marie and Aunt Jean, Mum's best friend, were outside waiting. Marie had raced to the hospital in Dad's bright yellow Cortina picking up Aunt Jean and Janis from Markington on the way. When we went out they both fell apart.

Marie had gone through that slightly rebellious teenager phase and she and Mum had some small spats but she had got very close to Mum in the weeks before we lost her. I know she is forever grateful for having had that two people time with her.

Marie says *"I 'ad a fortnights leave from the RAF and I spent it with Mum. One day we went to Semer Water, it was lovely. We got some bread buns and ham but we didn't 'ave any butter. We sat and ate 'em looking out over Semer Water. Then when we kem back we picked blue flowers. Mum loved blue flowers. it were the week she died"*

None of us could understand why no-one had seen it coming. Why didn't the doctors know? Luckily Terry stopped Marie going into the hospital and would not let her drive home as she was so upset. Marie says *"I deal with people going through that now and my heart bleeds for them"*

MUM

She was a remarkable lady, my Mum.
She suffered greatly and was never glum,
with seven children and husband to reckon,
common sense and humour prevailed to beckon
us all to follow her exemplary way

She managed with us all through tragedy
and for all our troubles gave the remedy.
Backbone of the family business she
was a housewife and mother and secretary
and the mainstay of life in the family

Illness was the cross she had to bear,
She bore it with dignity and love to share.
Only the good die young so they say.
Life is so unfair, and that was the way,
We love her; she is gone, only fifty-three

I wrote this shortly after Mum died. The last line does not quite fit but
it is so very heartfelt.

Three Men and a Story

On the 25th January 2011 Frank Dean, Peter Chadwick and Terry Thorpe all came to Lister House to sit with me and Dad, where he was now a resident and we reminisced. So many years had passed yet the memories were still fresh. It was a bit of fun to say the least but not all can go into the book to spare some blushes.

Frank, Peter and Terry T. talking of old times and having fun doing it

Frank

Frank the elder statesman, now seventy seven years old, is a talented writer and raconteur well known in Nidderdale. He has written several small books which are based on Dales and Dale's folk which are clever, amusing and anecdotal. He has held many evenings wherein he has done a recital of some of his work and has had his audience in stitches. He embraces a broad Yorkshire accent which enhances his delivery with a vengeance. He is a lovely man who has not lost his sense of humour.

Frank started working for Dad in 1949 after Tommy Newbould got him the job. One of his first memories was at Dad and Mums bungalow at Smelthouses before the move to Dacre. Frank said *"Len begged a cigarette off Betty and when she gave him one 'e flashed 'is packet of cigarettes in front of 'er. Betty without more ado, floored him, she sat on 'im and got the cigarette back. She didn't take prisoners didn't Betty, it were well funny"*

Frank worked in the workshop Dad had acquired in Dacre and when they moved to the house at Dacre Banks the workshop was transferred to the large cellar area of the house and the other workshop building was used for storage.

Frank remembers Miss Petty next door *"she warra bit of a tartar. She reckoned Len were diggin' up all 'er foundations. If ever we mentioned 'er to Len it were like red rag to a bull.*

*Your Terry, when 'e were around five years old, used t'get up to some right mischief yunnow. 'e used to play on top of t'pit. (*vehicle mending pit*). We were charged with keeping an eye on 'im if 'e were in't workshop area and we kept tellin' 'im it were dangerous but 'e took no 'eed. Well 'e fell down it* *eventually – naturally your Mum gave us what for. Another time, at Pateley this were, 'e had a lump of wood across the top of the stone water trough and 'e were jumping up and down on it. 'e were showing off and said it were strong enough. Well it weren't and 'e fell in and 'urt 'is leg. That'll teach 'im we thought. It didn't."*

There were of course some japes that the men got up to and Frank can recall some of them.

Apparently they were once working at the Grantley Hall near Ripon and they managed to get Frank in the front bucket of the digger. Naturally one of them raised it up and left him there for a short while. This was typical tomfoolery. They were also known to hot wire a vehicle so that the next driver in got a small electric shock.

They took their fun a bit far one day though, this time with Marie when she was about four years old, in the joiner's shop at Pateley. She used to wander all over and nowhere was off limits to her even if it was supposed to be. She ventured upstairs into the workshop looking for something to occupy her. Frank said *"she's lookin' for somethin' to lake with, let's give 'er somethin'"* John Kendrew gave her an old tin of paint, with some still in and with the lid dutifully removed. They also gave her a paint brush. Marie was well suited and charged off back into the house. Mum made a storming entrance into the workshop and there was hell to pay. She said *"if you ever do that again I'll sack you"* Frank says *"I thought – not again"*

Frank was laughing wholeheartedly while he related all these memories.

After five years he felt the need to enlist and he went into the forces for a term of three years. Dad apparently wasn't overly happy that he had enlisted for three years as two was the norm but Frank wanted to be in the medics and that required a three year stint. Dad kept his job open for him while he was away. Frank came back in 1957 and stayed with Dad until 1961 when he left and went into social work.

"the hours of work were eight till five and eight till twelve thirty on a Saturday in winter with an 'alf hour earlier start in summer. My biggest problem were the bus as I lived in Pateley and 'ad to get the bus 'ome. On a

*night I 'ad to get back to Summerbridge for twenty five past five to catch the
No. 23 top road bus. But the No. 24 bottom road bus kem past Dacre Banks
and the bus stop were right outside but it came at exactly six minutes to five.
Len wouldn't let me leave early to catch it so I were stuck with the walk. I used
to think to misself I were missin' the other bus just for the sake of six minutes
but that's just the way it was in them days"*

The first funeral Dad had in was for Harry Ascough who was the
Station Master at Dacre. *"I were very interested in the funeral side of the
business and I allus used to go wi Len to put people in coffins. 'e used to get
me back in on an evening to do it and I used to get two shillin's and sixpence
(12.5p today) for doing it. Len said it shouldn't 'ave been anythin' cos I should
be glad to learn off 'im! If the job were in normal working 'ours of course I did
not get any extra. Len used to write it on the timesheets as a 'putting in job'. If
funerals were out of normal 'ours I got five shillin's for that. I allus remember
your Dad as being very smart when he led funerals"*

Frank continues *"I will 'ave to tell you about the day 'e sacked me. What
'appened is it were after I'd come out of the forces. I had a pal who I 'ad been
best man for and 'e were comin' to spend a weekend wi me. We were working
on Jagger's bungalow up Greenhow at time. Well my pal 'ad never been to
Pateley before and 'e were due in Pateley at 11.30 off t' bus and I really wanted
to meet 'im. But we worked till 12 on a Sat'day, so in the morning I thought
I'd ask Len if he didn't mind me leaving early. I knew I'd 'ave to make me
own way down from Greenhow where we were working and I just wanted to
okay it wi Len so that I could leave to go meet 'im you see. Anyway when I got
to t' yard for some reason or other Len 'ad gone off to Arrigut* (Harrogate) *– an
early start to Beardmore Dobson's for supplies so I couldn't ask 'im you see cos
'e wasn't there. I though oh dear now what, I wanted to leave early. Anyway
up at Jagger's I left about quarter past eleven and I can't recall who gave me a
lift into Pateley but I just made it in time for this bus. However I reckon there
'ad been a bit of argy bargy brought up about it, though I don't know this for
sure, but in the afternoon Len sacked mi for leavin' without permission. And
I didn't really get chance to explain. Anyway after that I cleared off back down
to Weston Super Mare which is where I'd been previously stationed when I
were in t'RAF. When I got back home there warra letter waiting for me from*

Betty. She said it's very sad after all these years. Mi mother said there's also a message for you, you've got to ring Geoffrey Harper the vicar. I rang Geoffrey and 'e said to come round and see 'im. I thought – 'e's going to be trying to talk me into going back and I'm not givin' way I'm not going back.

Anyway when I went to see him he said –

You know Lens upset about you going I've been speaking to him.

Well I am too, I said, but I didn't do anything seriously wrong.

Well, he said, but strictly speaking Frank was you wrong to leave without permission early?

Well, I mean, I waited.

Never mind you waited, was you wrong?

So I says – strictly speaking I suppose I was but I couldn't ask 'im 'e wasn't there.

Well 'e might not admit it to you but 'e's a bit upset as well why not go round and tell 'im you're sorry.

I'm not going back 'e sacked me, that's it.

'e said – I'm not asking you t'go back just go round and admit that you were wrong.

Well I went round and I said – I'm just comin' t'say Len I'm sorry if I offended you –and I never mentioned going back.

and 'e said – well I am after all this time but you were wrong Frank so there's no point in tekkin issue.

I said – I know Len but I've tried to explain but I accept that I'm wrong.

Len said – well what you doing now?

I said – I don't know.

He said – well you might not want your job back but if you want it back you can start. Would you want to come back again?

I said – yes I would.

He said – well come in on Monday morning.

– And I went back and told Geoffrey Harper what 'ad 'appened but I think he'd set it up in t' first place. 'e said yes well you'll find it's hard cos the others

will probably stand laughing at yuh for crawling back yuh know but to walk in and do it is a lot braver than them standing laughing at yuh. Anyway on Monday morning I went in and there were a strange atmosphere for half an 'our then it all settled down. By it were a rum do but I were glad I were back"

Another funny do Frank recalls was *"Len 'ad a dark green Ford van and one day Arthur Kendrew were drivin' it and I were sat at side of 'im. Well I started to tap mi foot. Arthur said 'what's that noise? There's somethin' wrong wi this van, Len's vehicles allus 'ave somethin' wrong with 'em'. Well I kept it up all t'way t'Pateley. Arthur launched into Len when we got back and said it were faulty. I never did tell 'im.*

It were not allus me in t'japes, t'others did their fair share too"

After doing social work Frank left and went to work in the pharmacy stores at Harrogate General hospital and he took early retirement from there as he got a decent pay-out which he felt he could not turn down.

He did however get into some part-time work about twenty years ago by default but which in due course managed to upset Len quite unreasonably. A funeral director down the lower end of the dale asked him to help out at a couple of funerals and Frank jumped at the chance. He received a letter afterwards asking him if he would like to be more involved and, if so, could they call on him. Len was quite put out that Frank was working part-time for a rival even though he hadn't worked for Len for over twenty years. Len was cool with Frank for a long while but after Len became ill Frank visited him, after encouragement from others, and the two men shook hands thank goodness.

Terry joined them at the tender age of fifteen as Frank's apprentice.

Terry T.

Terry Thorpe, from now on referred to as Terry T so as not to be confused with Len's son, is a well-travelled gentleman. Frank said that Terry was a shy lad when he joined them but he soon got into the way of things.

Terry said *"I joined Len as Frank's apprentice in September 1953 when I were fifteen. I enjoyed the work and took great pride in making the coffins which were really quite beautiful. They were made and highly polished to a good sheen, then they were lined in satin type fabric. The furniture fixed to the outside were first class. Allus seemed such a shame for them to be buried. As time went on I did a lot of paintin' and decoratin' as well. We all turned our 'and to different jobs all in accordance with the work that kem in.*

I remember once Len had gone to take sizes for a funeral and when we asked 'im what they were, so that we could get on with making the coffin, 'e said 'two and three quarter 'ankies' which totally stumped us. Then 'e got out 'is anky and pulled it at opposite corners and said 'see, two and three quarter 'ankies' – 'e 'ad forgotten to take a tape measure with 'im.

I wasn't a big prankster but I did get in bother once though. Jim fisher used to tek this three wheeler 'ome to Summerbridge, doodlebug we called it. One evening I was in the street (High Street) and saw 'im coming down and gave 'im the 'V' sign, only it wasn't Jim it were Betty. She called me in next morning and gave me a right rollocking and told me if I did that again I'd be sacked. I were convinced it were Jim Fisher when I did it but I said nowt to Betty and just took her tellin' off, it got a big laugh for rest of 'em.

I remember when Len got t'job of t'cinema to pull down – that were very sad. All us young 'uns 'ad some good memories from there.

I left in 1978 and went t'work for the West Yorkshire Road Car Company – the Yorkshire red bus company for the next thirteen years. When WYRCC sold out it were split and Mr. Stephenson, who had worked for WYRCC, bought the property side. I then worked for him for the following twelve years. Mr Stephenson owned properties in Arrigut (Harrogate), *Leeds, Newcastle and the Lake District so I got to work all over the place. He eventually sold off a lot of his properties.*

Now I keep fit by still dancing on a regular basis and I go regularly with 'the lads' to Ripon for a curry. I haven't given up travelling though and have been all over the world. It's good to travel but it's good to come home"

Works Dinner 1958

Frank Dean, Peter Chadwick, Tommy Thackeray, Jack Richmond, Alf Hardcastle and Jimmy Fisher
Terry isn't on this picture as he was taking it.

Terry says *"Jim and Alf were funny, they used to measure their overtime in pints – three and half pints were the usual"*

Peter

Peter started working for Len in 1957. He was a county cricketer and played for Yorkshire and Len always let him have time off for matches. Len was quite proud that one of his men played for Yorkshire.

Peter said *"When I kem out of the RAF I took casual work until I could find a job plumbing. Mi father used to be a plumber and mi Uncle Jim was a plumber working for Stan Light. I 'ad done three years at night school prior to doing national service"*

Len has now joined our little tete a tete and is determined to put his oar in and adds *"Peter were planting trees when 'e kem out of t'air force and the vicar 'ad a word with me about 'im. So I thought a bit and said 'well when you see 'im tell 'im to come and see me. Peter kem and we chatted in mi office and I asked 'im what 'e wanted to do. When 'e told me I said that 'e couldn't come as an apprentice cos 'e couldn't live properly on t'wage but asked 'im if 'e would be prepared to come as a labourer on labourers rate, which was 'igher, but still do plumbing and finish off the remaining two years of 'is City and Guilds. He were well-schooled as 'e'd been to the Technical School and 'e finished 'is course. When 'e kem with 'is certificate I said to 'im 'that's it then Peter you're on full rate now"*

Peter said *"the funniest story I remember about Len is when 'e got the job of repairing the very pointed spire roof, with weather vane on top, of Castlestead"*

Castlestead is an unusual and many roofed, ornate building nestling in the bottom of the valley between Glasshouses and Pateley and can be seen from the main road above. The roof in question is very obvious and not something to be ascended certainly without hard hats, and by the look of it crampons.

Peter says *"Ken 'ad put scaffolding round the base of the roof and we were trying to work out 'ow we were going to get up to the weathercock on top. While we were discussing this Len, without further ado, started to crawl up the very steep incline of the roof. It were about fifteen feet and slated. Well by the time we'd finished talkin' e' were up you see. But he were not there long. 'e started to slide down. 'e were on 'is back with 'is feet down and 'e started driftin' down slowly. Well Len 'ad braces on, 'is braces caught on a bit of spoutin' bracket and 'e hung there with 'is trousers 'unched up. Oh it were funny. We got 'im back on t'scaffolding and Ken asked 'im if 'e were alright. 'Course I'm alright what's up wi' you' Len said. It were only t'strength of 'is braces and t'brackets that saved 'im. 'e could 'ave dropped off more than twenty feet. But that were typical of Len"*

"Len 'ad no fear. 'e used to test spark plugs by 'oldin' them. You wouldn't catch me 'oldin' a live spark plug. You get a pretty big jolt off 'em.

Another incident were when we were buildin' some bungalows at Summerbridge. Len were a bit late in comin' t'pick us up and, Newby, Len's dad worked for 'im at the time and as 'e only lived in Low Laithe 'e used 'is bike to get 'ome. So at five o'clock Newby set off 'ome. Len eventually arrived to drive us back to Pateley. Anyway we caught Newby up just as 'e were getting to 'is 'ouse and Len did a not-too-smart move and pulled a swerve in front of 'im. Newby couldn't stop and drove straight into t' back of us. By Newby didn't 'alf 'ave a go at Len for that – there were 'eck on"

Peter left and went to work for the Water Board around 1968 to work as an inspector. There were a lot of lead pipes in those days thus there were also a lot of leaks to search out so, he was kept very busy. He retired from the Water Board at sixty but stayed on a part-time basis with the grand title of Plumbing Bye-law Inspector. He gave this up when they asked him to relocate his work and go to Hull to sort out the removal of lead pipes from domestic properties. He was with the Water Board some twenty years in total.

"Well that were one step too far for me" he says *'So now I do nowt'*

Frank the Literary Man

Franks literary expertise did not go unnoticed in the dales and his entertaining evenings were a great success and he has allowed me to include one of his tales – it is called 'My Friend Chad'. So it is rather obvious who he is talking about.

My friend, Chad was a plumber by trade but he was more noted for his cricket. One Saturday he received a call from the local doctor requesting him to pop up and repair the toilet that was not flushing properly. Chad protested that he was about to set off for an away match so the toilet repair would have to wait. "Now look here", said the doctor, "When you ring for me, I come straight away, and I expect you to make an immediate response to my plea". "Alright" says Chad, and a few minutes later he was ringing the doctor's door bell. When the doctor opened the door Chad said "Where's that troublesome toilet?". The doctor showed him upstairs to the bathroom. Chad took one look at the toilet pan. He then pulled out two tablets from his jacket pocket, dropped them into the toilet pan and said to the doctor, "Now then, if it's not better by Monday morning give me another ring".

Well done Chad if it's true and well done Frank if it's not !

The following is actually a tale that Frank was given over 40 years ago and I am delighted to be able to include it.

A young couple went to buy a house in the country. When they returned they realised they had not seen the W.C. They wrote to the Vicar asking him where it was. The Vicar, being ignorant of the term "W.C.", thought it meant Wesleyan Chapel; imagine their surprise when they received the following letter:

Dear Mr. X.,

I regret that I must inform you that the nearest W.C. is ten miles away. This is unfortunate if you are in the habit of attending regularly. It may interest you to know that many people take their lunch and make a day of it. By the way, it is made to accommodate 1,000 people, and it has been decided to replace the wooden seats with plush ones to ensure comfort for those who have had to wait a long time for proceedings to begin. Ladies are presided over by the Vicar who gives them all the help they need; all children sit together and sing throughout the proceedings. The last time my wife went was twelve months ago, and she had to stand through proceedings as it was so crowded. Hoping this will be of use, and trusting that you will attend regularly.

Yours truly,

Vicar.

P.S. Hymn sheets will be found behind the door – please return them after use.

Frank related these, and very many other tales, in real fruit of the moors broadest of Yorkshire accents.

Courtesy of Frank Dean from his publication 'The Magic of Nidderdale' some past and present memories published in 1983

Eggy and Paul

After the very fruitful session with Frank, Terry and Peter that yielded some 'reet grand' memories I soon realised that the men who worked for Dad had some wonderful tales to tell. There were very many men who had worked for Dad over the years, some having much longer service than others. The firm of 'L N Watson – Building Contractor and Funeral Director' spanned at least 45 years with the funeral business continuing thereafter. Frank, Terry and Peter, all with very many years service, were early employees. Ian Eglin (aka Eggy) and Paul Ripley came along a bit later and they too worked for him for many years.

Eggy started as an apprentice joiner in 1974. He was still at school and he came on work experience on Mondays and Wednesdays.

Eggy: "*I hated school and Len had got right busy. We were doing some council work on the schools at the time so Len had an agreement with Joe Turner, the Headmaster, that I could work more than two days a week. I finished up working full time even though I hadn't left school. You wouldn't do that now would yuh. I worked for Len for over eighteen years until 1992*"

Paul started as a labourer in 1977. He was working for a company called Tankfit, which was a small engineering firm in Pateley Bridge, but he hated the work because he was cooped up inside all day and all he wanted to do was work out of doors. He saw an advert saying 'labourer wanted' in the Pateley paper (aka Pateley Bridge and Nidderdale Herald) on a Friday.

Paul: *"after work I went along and knocked on Len's door and said I've come about the job I've seen advertised. Len asked me when I could start and could I start Monday. I said that I would have to work a week's notice. Len said, right, the job's yours. So that was my interview! Obviously it were because I had known Len and his family for many years, and I used to play in his yard with Terry and Dave Gamble, so he knew me pretty well anyway. It took about two minutes did that interview and I stayed for about eight years. I started off as a labourer but if you were keen to learn then Ken Batty would teach you. I'm glad he did really"*

When Eggy started it was to replace John Sturdy who had recently left. Eggy remembers men that were in the firm at the time included old Billy Williams, Alan Buck (aka Bucky), Little Danny Riddler, Peter Kent and young Nigel.

Eggy: *"Nigel used to travel all the way from Pudsey on a moped and he were never late, even in winter. He were a witness to that Barry Prudom murderer in 1982 who shot and killed many people including policemen and held people hostage. It were a big police hunt for Prudom and Nigel had seen him near Fewston Reservoir which is near where he shot one of the policeman David Haigh. The police kept coming to take Nigel away for interviews. He were invited to a presentation when Prudom were caught"*

Eggy: *"I'll tell you what, we learned everything, I mean I were a joiner but I learned everything. When I first started it were just mainly joinery work but as time went on, and we had to take on such a variety of jobs, we got to do other things. We were never bored. Len would take on any job no matter what size nor even for that matter how high a building were that we had to work on. He wasn't scared of anything. He would never say 'No we don't do that' There were times when we all thought 'oh no it's too big for us' but Len wouldn't turn anything away. He kept us in work"*

There were few builders in the dale at the time – 'the Watsons' and 'the Foxtons' and Lee & Holmes.

Eggy: *"it's different now int it. Everybody works for themselves rather than for a company. We definitely got some experience working for Len"*

Paul: *"we did undertaking to roofing, pipelines to whole buildings"*

I asked them both about any japes that were 'got up to' while they worked for Dad.

Paul: *"what was your initiation into the firm Eggy?"*

Eggy: *"I can't say that"* he said blushing slightly. *"but I do remember on a job down at New York Mills Terry T. And Bucky squirted a full bottle of washing up liquid down my trousers. And I'll tell you what, don't believe what they say about it being kind to hands cos it isn't kind to something else! I were red raw. I tell you what when you look back at some of the stuff, when you were an apprentice, well it just wouldn't happen these days would it, but it were the done thing then"*

Old Billy Williams was a real character and was not prone to personal cleanliness and always had beard stubble. They all knew it and accepted it because that was how he was. He was however a bit mean to Eggy when he first started. He used to give him 'chin pie' (aka 'whisker pie' – rubbing your chin against someone else's face) which was akin to harsh sandpaper being rubbed on your face.

Young Jonathan Wardman started on work experience with Eggy but did not go on to take a full time job. It is not really surprising with the ribbing he got.

Paul: *"We were working at the Railway Cottages which were not far from the High Street. Bucky used to like vanilla slices and he wanted Jonathan to get him some. Well Jonathan had been sent for stuff before and had forgotten half of the order so Bucky wrote on a huge piece of plasterboard. Poor Jonathan went all the way over by the river side with it in his shoulder and he propped it up on the counter at Hagenbach's bakery shop. He were doing what he were told"*

Eggy: "*The first job I worked on were at the Drill Hall in Bridgehousegate. We were converting it into flats. Well we were plaster boarding on the first day and I remember Bucky asking Jonathan if he liked heights. Jonathan said no not really. So Bucky teased 'im about it. We still managed to take it all in good spirit though, you had to really*"

Eggy: "*There were one day however that were very funny. An architect came to look round and he opened the airing cupboard just as Jonathan's feet came through the ceiling, all he could see were his feet hanging down. Couldn't have timed it better. Poor Jonathan – they set him on glazing a door with fifteen panes of glass in it and he managed to break thirteen with the nails – we were only very young at the time*"

Eggy: "*Bucky had Jonathan in his sights but Old Billy allus had me in his sights. He once nailed my dinner bag to a chair. We all had dinner bags in them days. I got a bit braver then though and thought I'd cap the bugger. He always used to read the Yorkshire Post in his break. He would spread it out fully in front of him to read it. So I put a match to it as he were reading it and it went straight up! Well he chased me. I nearly broke my leg over this. We had cut a hole out for a new staircase and the old one were still in. I ran up the old one and I thought he were after me up the stairs as I could hear this tapping. So I jumped for the ladder at the other side and missed it properly and caught mi shin so badly I thought I'd broken mi leg. We apprentices were fair game but that was how it was*"

There was a natural progression of hierarchy in the joiners shop.

Eggy: "*There were a little black pot-bellied stove in the joiners shop which were a good thing cos it were blooming cold in winter. Well the longer you had been there the nearer you got to it. You worked your way round the benches. Thorpy had been there longest so his vice were the nearest, right next to the stove, Bucky were next and I were right over the other side. My back were frozen in winter. Anyway I worked my way round. That's how it worked*"

Work was never stopped for harsh weather unless it was totally impossible to work, and such conditions were a winter certainty. They were once working at a cottage up at Heyshaw in the snow. It was the only job that they had in at the time and needs must. They carried materials up from the main road to the cottage in snow up to their waists and it *"were 'ard going"* said Eggy. *"We wouldn't do that today"* One winter was so bad however, that work had to be stopped for four days and they were all sent home. It was so cold they could not stand it. There was a big water trough in the yard that the men used for cleaning tools and spades. This was two feet deep and it froze solid that winter.

Pateley Bridge over the years was subjected to a bit of flooding. Work still had to go on whenever possible.

Eggy: *"it used to flood Millfield Street and it would sneak up into the yard. Terry T told me he once kem down the steps in the joiners shop to see all the wood shavings floating about. This were before my time"*

Paul: *"I lived in Millfield Street and I've seen it up to the top of my Mum's fireplace. Once it had flooded and my Dad were coming home off the eight o'clock bus. Well our street were deep in water so Len got his JCB out and he got my Dad in the front bucket and drove it along our street. We were in the upstairs rooms as downstairs were under water and mi Dad tapped on the window. We opened it and he climbed out of the bucket into the bedroom. Len also used to use that JCB to pull feast wagons out of the feast field (at Pateley fair in September) cos it used to be right muddy when it had rained. That JCB were Len's pride and joy"*

Paul: *"your Terry were allus tinkering about with stuff. I once kem into the yard and he were tinkering with a lawn mower. He said put your finger on that and I did as he asked, it was onto the spark plug and he pulled the cord and I got a right shock"*

Eggy: *"Chris Calvert were the main practical joker though. He would hot wire from a spark plug to pick up through the seat and when you got in to start it you got a shock"*

Paul: *Aye everyone knew Len used to make 'is tea bags last for two drinks and one morning 'e got up to see a string of teabags all pegged out on the washing line in t'back yard. That were Chris! Len took it in good stead"*

A job for complete refurbishment of a hairdressing shop in Ripon was taken on. This involved removal of some internal walls, new ceilings, electrics, plumbing and plastering – the usual gamut.

Eggy: *"one day the architect arrived for a meeting with Len. I remember it were a right nice day. Well this bloke kem in wearing a leather jacket, helmet and scarf and started wandering around. We though who the hell is this? It were Len – he'd only gone and bought himself a Triumph Bonneville motorbike. It were quite funny really cos we were beginning to get a bit protective of the firm seeing a stranger wandering about the site"*

Paul: *"Chris Calvert took a wagon load of rubbish to the tip and he found a shop window manikin and he brought it back. It were funny when he got back, with this naked manikin sitting on the seat next to him. He were proud as punch with it. Anyway he sat it on the shop toilet out of the way. Len arrived not long after and first thing he did was go to the toilet. As he opened the door he saw the legs and he quickly shut it and said sorry. He asked us who the lady was in there. That were right funny"*

By this time Paul and Eggy had lost all sense of propriety that was obvious when we first started this interview and were little short of rolling about the floor laughing.

An earlier job they had was working on a barn property at Dacre Top. Eggy and George Earney were working together on a gable end. They had a pair of steps with a couple of planks strung across which was a usual configuration to create a platform.

Eggy: *"we were cutting holes out for joists and we heard this rumbling noise and the filling in the cavity were dropping down in the wall. Then suddenly there were a right crash and all the lot fell in. I sort of jumped backwards off the plank to where the door was. Bucky and some others were working on another job across the main road and I ran over and said George is under all that heap of stuff he might be dead. It were the whole gable end that 'ad come down. I said you'll have to come he's under it all – I were panicking. Well we were scrambling about trying to move stone trying to find him and then someone tapped me on the shoulder. I jumped and said 'how the hell did you get out of there?' He said 'I just saw daylight, just a chink of light and I jumped towards it'. The only damage was I had a bruise from a stone hitting me on the back. George were well lucky. The following day Len landed with some 'ard 'ats (hard hats) cos he were worried that Health and Safety might come and he said we 'ad to wear 'em. We wore 'em for about two days then put 'em aside cos they were so uncomfortable. That were a close do though"*

Paul: *"the only other Health and Safety issue were at that same hairdressers in Ripon. They visited the site and said we were using mains electric and we should be using 1.10. It stopped the job for a day and they said they were coming back to check but they didn't"*

Paul: *"Colin Chandler had a close call once didn't he? They'd been working up by Old St Mary's Church high up the hill and Len's pride and joy, his JCB, were there. He asked Colin to bring it back to the yard. Well as he were coming down the hill, it were pretty steep, the brakes weren't holding and they got away with him. Colin couldn't go straight down as it ran into the High Street so he put his bucket down on the road and used it to slow him down. He ran it into the kerb by St. Mary's estate taking up six kerbstones and he managed to stop. All the tools kem hurtling forward in the cab. He were well lucky he wasn't hurt"*

Eggy and Colin were given a job of building a garage at the back of the church in Pateley. Their job brief included a stern instruction not to damage an apple tree that was in the middle of the lawn as it was the owners pride and joy.

Eggy: *"it were our last day and the job had gone well. We had the wagon there and were putting topsoil on the lawn and I got a bit far back with the wagon. The tree got caught in the tow bar bracket and it were smashed to bits. All that were left was a stem, one branch, a leaf and one little apple. That were it. So Colin said 'tell him that a plague of locusts kem and we tried to fight em off with shovels and it didn't work' and we started laughing. Anyway we went back to the yard and Len kem out with the wages and he thought something were up. He said 'what's up with you two?' 'Well we've got something to tell you – you know that apple tree' – well all I could think of when I were trying to tell him was this plague of locusts and I started laughing and we were rolling on the floor in the workshop laughing. Len said 'it int bloody funny he's going to go crackers, Len were going mad and that made us laugh more, we couldn't help it. By it were funny"*

Paul: *"on that same job Len had been to the quarry for some hardcore and he parked it on the hill'.* Eggy: *'yes and my car were parked further down. He kem in and asked where we wanted it putting. Just then a lady kem in and said 'excuse me – is that wagon yours?' Len said yes. 'well it's just run away and it's hit that car' I thought oh no! Len said Nooo it can't a done. Well I were a bit annoyed and I said 'no she's making it up Len' But it had. It had felled a lamp post and smashed back of my car to bits. Apparently the hand brake had gone on it"*

Money was often very tight and saving money in whatever way possible was paramount in keeping the business afloat. Unless a vehicle failed it did not get attention. It almost became a joke to the men but it was obviously not conducive to maintenance of Health and Safety.

Paul: *"we used to be worn out on a morning didn't we? Them vehicles – you pushed 'em out of the yard, down the lane, round the bus station and back to see if you could start 'em. If you got one started you used that to tow the others off!"*

Eggy: *"Oh I'll tell you another cracker. Len had an old Simca van. Me and George kem out of the yard one day, I were driving and we got to the bottom of the street* (High Street) *and there were a police car went over the bridge. Well like an idiot I followed it. We got the big wave over by the police. Well I knew that one of the tyres were a bit dodgy and I leaned against the vehicle at that corner in the hope he wouldn't see it. He said 'don't worry about that lad I've already seen that'. He said 'you do realise your tax is out don't you?' Anyway who should pass then but Len on his way to the garage and he waved as if nothing were 'appening. He got his petrol and waved again on his way back. This copper said 'I think we'd better go see your boss' so we went back to the yard. We went into the office and Len said 'we're in for it now' I said 'aye – this fella wants a word with you. Len did get fined for it"*

Dad did everything he possibly could rather than pay someone unnecessarily. He did all his own sign writing which he took huge pride in. He used to sit on a five gallon drum with a cushion and he used a cane with a ball covered in material (puff stick) to steady his hand. He had books with letters in of different fonts which he used to copy. He was even known to produce some architectural plans on occasions.

Paul: *"yes he were very careful with his money. He hated competition and he found out that another funeral director had got some little pencils with his name on. Len said 'Bowers have got some pencils get round to the shops and get the poshest pencils you can find' Well we did and then Len cut them up into three! When we did a funeral, I can't remember how many bits of pencil there were, but Len had counted 'em and three were missing! That had us in stitches"*

Paul: *"I'll tell you what though you allus got your money. It must have been hard, we've often said that"*

Paul: *"I remember driving the hearse – we went to Stonefall cemetery and coming back Len said 'knock it out of gear' – it were to save petrol"*

Eggy: *"I used to drive the hearse and I were so little then I could hardly see over the bonnet!"*

One thing that Dad took very seriously was his funeral business. He administered that with utmost propriety. If ever a funeral came in where the deceased was not in a good condition for whatever reason, be it accident or otherwise, he did his best not to involve any of the men and dealt with any slightly unnerving task himself. The men knew this and appreciated it.

Eggy: *"Terry Thorpe kept a list reverently on the joiners shop wall of every funeral and date that had come in. I only ever helped make one coffin and it were awful cos it were a childs, after that coffins were bought in ready-made. The handmade ones were better though"*

Eggy : *"One 'pick up' as Len called it was to collect a man who were very large – he were seven feet tall. We really struggled, we got him half way down the stairs and in the end Len said we'll have to stand him up to get him round the corner. He were still on the stretcher and we stood him up and managed it"*

Dad went off playing with Lofthouse and Middlesmoor Brass Band on several occasions throughout the year.

Paul: *"all us workmen looked forward to the annual Tan Hill do when Len went off to play with Lofthouse and Middlesmoor Brass Band – we knew it would be any easy day. Also Kilnsey Show as he'd be off for that day as well – we didn't take advantage but we did take it easy!"*

Eggy: *"Len used to get his trumpet out at Christmas do's. He would also get out an accordion and his mouth organ. Provided his own cabaret so to speak! We've had some good do's"*

Paul: *"We used to go on the odd trip to the coast. We did it for three or four years. There were Thorpy, Old Bill and Bob Kirkley. We used to stop off in York on the way back and I remember Old Bill in a nightclub there. He said 'what sort of bloody row is this?' We laughed ourselves silly at Old Bill in there"*

Eggy: *"I've another tale about drinking. We were working on a right big House on Cavendish Avenue in Arrigut* (Harrogate) *and Ian Burns were doing the painting. We were working away and the lady of the house kem out and asked where Ian was. Ian had said he were just nipping up into town at dinner time to look at another job. Anyway it got to four o'clock and this lady kem out again. She said she was going to show Ian some colours for paint and she said he 'hasn't been to see me yet' We had to tell her we didn't know where he was. Anyway just as we said that there were a rustling noise and Ian fell through the hedge absolutely blathered out of his head. I said Oh I'm sorry I don't think you'll be choosing paint today. Shouldn't have laughed but it were too funny"*

Paul: *"we once went to the Half Moon at Fellbeck for Christmas dinner. You know what's coming don't you Eggy? Well Len said 'you can have anything off the menu' well, we thought, this is all right. But Len were a bit deaf and didn't really know how loud he was talking and he spoke to the girl behind the counter and said – tell 'em the steaks off. We were creased up at that one"*

Eggy: *"Aye and we never got our holiday money until after our holiday. He said it were just so you had something to come back to. Even at Christmas you had to go back during the week after to get your money"*

Paul: *"you allus got your money though. We've often said when we worked for ourselves – how he managed to get all those wages together each week we don't know. We know how hard it is"*

Eggy: *"Aye it must have been hard. I'll tell you what I'll never have anyone working for me, the hassle he must have had"*

Paul: *"I remember him being short of work and we spent two weeks tidying up the workshop in the yard. We couldn't throw anything away so we were just moving things around from one place to another. He didn't send you home. That must have been hard"*

Eggy: *"We got laid off one Christmas. He said 'I'm sorry I've never done it before but I'm going to have to lay you off. He'd never laid anyone off in all of twenty years. So me and another lad went down the job centre to sign on. When I got back home it had snowed. There were these welly prints at our back* door. *Well I knew it were Len cos he allus walks at quart t' three* (quarter to three). *So I rung him up and asked him what he wanted. He said 'how did you know it were me?' I said 'I've seen your footprints in the snow' He said 'how did you know they were mine?' I said 'cos you allus walk at quart t' three' He said he were coming to tell me that he'd got some more work on and we could come back tomorrow. So that were it – laid off for just one day in all the time I had been there"*

Paul: *"He used to give us a Christmas bonus"*

"Aye" laughed Eggy *"but he were a blooming good darts player and he'd come to the Christmas do and win it all back at darts!"*

Eggy and Paul are now rolling in laughter exercising feeble attempts to stay upright.

Paul: *"I'll tell you what though, those were some of the happiest times working there"*

Eggy: *"Yeah it were a good time"*

Times changed as the years progressed and more and more people were setting up working for themselves. Jobs for bigger firms that carried bigger overheads were becoming few and far between.

Paul: *"I was offered a job with George Lambert and I had to take it as it offered me more opportunity in view of the jobs coming in, but I were sad to leave"*

Eggy: *"I left to set up working for myself. It were sad to do but it was time"*

Paul and Eggy then went on to mention lots of men that had worked for Len.

Paul: *"blimey we're gonna run out of paper at this rate"*

Colin Chandler (junior), Eggy and Paul

Pushing Off Route

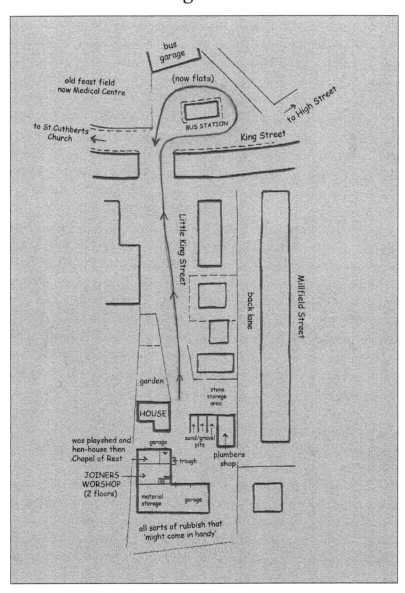

Pateley Bridge in flood mode

*The bottom of the High Street in the 60's and below in earlier years –
this is not as deep as it eventually became and caused much upheaval
for Pateley folk*

Pictures courtesy of Nidderdale Museum

All the dales men, and some from farther afield, who worked for Spanner over the years

Ken Batty (builder)

Paul Beckett

Michael Blakey (app.builder)

Alan Buck (joiner)

Ian Burns (painter)

Peter Chadwick (plumber)

Colin Chandler (Jnr –builder)

Frank Dean (joiner)

George Earney

Jim Fisher (builder/plaster)

Edwin Gamble

Andrew Gaunt (electrician)

Alf Hardcastle (labourer)

David Harris (decorator)

Clifford Hopkinson (labourer)

Arthur Kendrew senior (joiner)

Tony Kendrew (labourer)

Bob Kirkley (electrician)

Brian Lawson (labourer)

Tommy Newbould (joiner)

Danny Ridley (plumber)

Jockey Beckett

Maurice Blades (builder)

Walt Bradshaw (builder)

Dave Burns (painter)

Chris Calvert (labourer)

Colin Chandler Snr – builder)

Roger Davies (builder)

Ian Eglin (joiner)

Laurence Furniss (builder)

Roland Garner (labourer)

Philip Grayshon (labourer)

Charlie Harris (labourer)

Derek Hinds (labourer)

Earnest Kay (labourer)

John Kendrew junior (joiner)

Peter Kent (mechanic & plumber)

Nigel K. (apprentice)

Michael Lowe (app. Joiner)

Jack Richmond (builder)

Paul Ripley (labourer)

Harry Seed (labourer) Peter Shearstone (lbr/plumber)
Dave Simpson (painter) Mick Smith (joiner)
Michael Snow (labourer) Paul Spence (joiner)
John Storey (labourer) John Sturdy (joiner)
Tommy Thackeray (labourer) John Thorpe (joiner)
Terry Thorpe (joiner/decorator) Teddy Timlin (electrician)
Neil Watson (electrician) Newby Watson (labourer)
Terry Watson (builder) Terry White (joiner)
Ron Whiting (labourer) Billy Williams senior (labourer)
'Wiggy' Williams junior (labourer) and Mum and Me

With apologies for any names misspelled or anyone who has been missed off this list.

Spanner Calls Time......

There was no specific life defining moment when Dad decided to quit the building contracting. It was a slow build up of changes in the dale and the decline of work coming in. Times had changed and work for bigger firms was not prolific. One man bands were now the order of the day. He still kept on the funeral business side though this was not highly lucrative. Most unthoughtfully the dales folk did not seem to be popping their clogs so regularly.

Dad always valued his funeral business and had great pride in providing a service befitting the solemnity and propriety of the occasions.

There was a problem to this at one time however and that was instigated by the good old British telephone company – there was a mix up in the phone book. The problem was the two numbers that had got confused were – Dad's funeral business number and a local doctors.

He got a call once to a caravan. So he dutifully put on his best frock and got his funeral bag and set off. When he walked in the caravan he said *'ah, pr'aps it's not me you want'* – the man was sitting up in bed. He managed to extricate himself without spilling the beans to the poor unfortunate.

In later years Dad demolished the outbuildings, which was incredibly sad. So many memories were entrenched within.

The Joiner's Workshop

A small chapter has to be dedicated to the joiner's workshop. It was wonderful. I got chance, before it was demolished, to show it to my husband and am so very pleased I did. The memories flooded back. It was like stepping back in time to a stage set that would not have been out of place in Beamish Museum.

This building served a very different purpose originally. It was part of the property serving Scott Gate Ash – a stone quarry at the top of the hill on the east side of the valley. Parallel stone walls run vertically up the side of the valley to the quarry and railway lines ran between them down to the valley floor. The joiner's workshop was actually part of the winding shed that served this railway along with other buildings that have been incorporated in Hawksworth's yard.

The ground floor was littered with various mechanical and electrical tools. There was a large band saw with a huge wheel that, with lack of total attention could easily remove a finger without even coughing. The Health and Safety Executive had not been invented then, or if it had it certainly was not so vociferous nor as inanely powerful as today.

The main working area was on the second floor which was not exactly conducive to easy removal of the hand-crafted coffins. The workbench was long, solid and large with a drop channel that ran the length of it and had a vice on each corner. The best bit was the condition. It had a distressed finish and looked like it had been subjected to mass attack from trillions of chisels, creating an utterly exclusive patination.

Then there was 'the wall'. Oh how I remember looking at those rude postcards. Actually they were very amusing and there was always 'the calendar' which featured a monthly or annual lady in state of not total undress. Total undress was not acceptable then. The last calendar on the wall was dated 1972.

The 'ladies' on the postcards tended to be voluptuous in bosom, bottom or volume – one or all three, and the men depicted tended to be normal size or even weedy. Such would doubtless be branded as sexist now and would definitely have got coverage in our media. Columns would doubtless have been dedicated to same by the inordinately scathing and witty columnists who splatter our tabloids of today.

I think the joiner's wall was my first introduction to 'rudity'.

I dearly wish I had taken a picture of the workbench and the wall.

Dad Met a Lady Called Nancy....

Nancy used to work in 'the hut' which was a gentlemen's outfitters on Park Road in Pateley. Mum often used to go in there for clothes for Dad and Terry and have a natter.

Sometime after Mum died Dad became close friends with Nancy and they remained friends ever since. They took to travelling all over England and enjoyed some trips down to Cornwall. Dad had a caravan on a site

in Bridlington for quite some time and they often trotted off there. They eventually got a touring caravan and took that on English jaunts.

Nancy was a huge support to Dad during his declining years when he could not get about quite as much as he had been able to. They maintained separate homes but spent much time in each other's company and often ate out in various dales hostelries.

Nancy and Dad in Cornwall

Siblings in Later Years

None of us did too well in the marriage stakes in that we all had more than one marriage. However we produced some wonderful children between us.

Tony and I had two children – Sally and Richard. Unfortunately our marriage hit the rocks, after nineteen years and several businesses, and we called time. Now I am a very happy teddy bear. I have my health back, I live in Pudsey with the best man on the planet, I have my own photography studio and I write.

Jan and Pete were blessed with three children – Carl, Melanie and Gary. After their marriage split she went to London and actually became a train driver on a private line for a while. How cool is that! She was a very accomplished seamstress and had her own business for a while. Now married to Ray she lives in Knaresborough and has unfortunately suffered a debilitating illness but she still maintains a joy de vivre. Well she would wouldn't she – she is a Watson.

Marie and Dennis had two children – Daniel (Dan) and Natasha (Tash). They too were together many years and jointly ran the Crown Hotel in Pateley where Dennis has remained as mine host. She embarked on a whole new career after her first marriage and became an advanced ambulance technician. She is now married to Mark, a highly talented dry stone-waller and one of the few remaining with this skill.

Apparently Dad actually did some ambulance coverage in the 60's. They had nobody to cover nights at the time and Dad volunteered. It was a bit of a haphazard service in those days. Now and then he had to go out on his own without any medical assistance, though sometimes he managed to procure a nurse. One night he was called out to a patient up the dale who had suffered a perforated ulcer and was coughing up blood. He actually had to take the door off to get him downstairs to the ambulance. When he passed Blue Bell Woods the electrics in the ambulance failed and, as Spanner was at the helm, he managed to get it working again. However on the way back it did the same thing again in the very same place. No offence to Dad but it is good to know that the service is now in well trained hands and, just to keep it in the family, Marie's son Dan is also a paramedic.

Given half a chance I wouldn't have put it past Dad not to have left his business cards in the ambulance but that would have been a slight step too far!

When Marie and Mark were due to get married they arranged their reception at the Harefield Hall Hotel and just before their wedding day the hotel suffered a bad fire. A new venue had to be hastily arranged. Well where else could it be but the grand Memorial Hall that Jack built – sorry Dad built. Catering was provided at short notice magnificently by the culinary expertise of Jacko of the Royal Oak.

I got into poetic mode and wrote an amusing anecdotal poem for their reception and also I took the opportunity to resurrect the picture of the ceremony of the laying of the foundation stone in 1959. I blew up the print and added a footnote.

No expense was spared in the preparation for Marie and Mark's wedding reception. Len and his men worked round the clock to get the building completed on time !!

…. which naturally caused great amusement!

Terry and his first wife were blessed with three children. Terry was an excellent builder and gained accolades for his work some of which is evident in the dales. He eventually moved down to Cambridge where he still lives and where he met his lovely wife Linda who sports a South African accent to add more mix to all the family dialects.

Terry and Linda recently got married and held their reception at the newly rejuvenated Harefield Hall. Luckily the outer facade was not damaged in the fire and it is restored to the beautiful building inside and out that it always has been. The wedding was a steaming success and the hosts did them proud.

Ella lives on the south coast with her husband Neil with whom she has two children Jodie and Tiffany. She also has two children – Carrie and Amanda from a previous marriage. She was quite a career girl and became a Highways Manager.

Little Paula married Charles an officer in the American Air Force. They along with Jenny and James all live in Alabama. Paula worked for many years with disabled children with learning difficulties at which she excels and she still works with children.

I keep calling Paula little but she isn't. In fact I am the smallest of the lot of us.

Gilly Gliding

In May 1984 Tony and I and our children moved temporarily into a flat in Pateley Bridge whilst looking for a public house to run. We had sold our house and milk business in Harrogate and to fill in employment time Tony was working for Dad whilst we looked for our next business venture. Sally continued to attend school in Harrogate and Richard started school in Pateley Bridge and was at the age of enjoying the fruits of Dad's sandpit just as we all had in our childhood.

It was whilst we were living at Pateley that Richard in his wisdom took one of Dad's small ladders from the yard and carried it all the way up the High Street and put it against the Barclays bank window. The ladder was twice the size of Richard but he had a goal. He climbed the ladder to look in. Those inside got the shock of their lives to see a head appear at the window. It is laughed about now but it could have been a problem if they had thought they were about to have a smash and grab and someone had surreptitiously pressed that red button under the teller's counter and the PPST (Pateley Police Swat Team) had come swarming down the High Street. Perhaps a seven year old did not look quite like the average bank thief. Richard said he just wanted to know what was in there.

He had a slightly different view on the world did Richard. One of his serious childhood questions to me was "Mum? Were there dinosaurs when you were young?" Nice child.

So at the prehistoric age of 36, and still not fully aware of 'what my dad did in the war', Tony and I were on our way to Thirsk to look at a public house – the Blacksmiths Arms – that we were thinking of taking. This route took us past Dishforth airfield.

Well would you credit it? Flying would appear to be in the blood. I was awestruck, not with the pub (albeit we did take the pub) but with the gliders on the airfield we past. Gliders were flying and one was being winched off at a decidedly acute angle. I was hooked.

After speaking with my brother-in-law Dennis, who was ex RAF, I learned it was a forces gliding club but as he knew people there he could introduce me in the hope of a flight. Dennis kindly took me over one Sunday and introduced me to Ben Benoist his ex-superior in the RAF. Ben was chairman of Cleveland's and a rather good glider pilot with mountain flying experience. Dennis left as gliding was not his scene, but I stayed. I learned that there were two clubs on the site; Cleveland's was the forces club and Hambleton's was the civilian club and they only operated on weekends.

My first flight was brilliant and I was hooked and I knew this was something I had to learn to do. I sat around all day on the big red bus (a double decker bus that was used for relaxing in between flights, talking, eating and reading etc.). I watched as gliders landed and were pulled back onto line and others taking off and asked daft questions like '*what are the tyres for*' (they were for placing on a gliders wing when it was on the ground to prevent the wing lifting by a gust of wind). Obvious really. I tended to talk glider talk for the next few years and was doubtless quite a boring but totally invigorated person.

On the 6th May 1984 I joined Hambleton's gliding club and had my first training flight. I count myself very lucky that I had the crème de la crème of gliding expertise at my will for learning and what a wonderful way to learn to fly it was, with a pick of talented pilots. Sounds like a collective noun. The clubs boasted probably more instructors than any other club in England and the safety aspect was exceptional. I loved this regimented safety aspect that Dishforth embraced. There were so many instructors available, but I soon learned which one's I preferred to fly with and learn from. On 8th July 1984 I flew solo, I was that keen.

It is stupendous in the sky to work the lift and get so high
And what a wondrous thing is air to fly around with ne'er a care

I learned to fly in a Blanik which was a large metal glider with a forgiving nature and the requisite two seats one behind the other. The instructor took up the rear seat with the pupil up front. I loved flying so much that I walked around staring at the sky much to my family's chagrin. I was quite sad really. My regular verbiage of 'lift' and 'sink' and how it occurred must really have entertained them, not. I was often accused of looking for sinks in the sky. My bedtime reading evolved from 'who dunnits' to aeronautical charts. On the day of my first solo flight it was a beautiful day the sky was blue splattered with cumulus with lift popping up all over. After I released from the tug plane I gained height but then worried about being in trouble for keeping the glider up too long and started to lose height, then I thought *this is just too good* and I went back up again. When I landed and we pulled the glider back into line it was to applause from my now fellow glider pilots. That night, back at Pateley, I took my newly achieved wings down to the Crown pub tucked under my nose like a moustache. It was a good day.

Dishforth had workshop areas, bunkhouses, office, chart room, bar and kitchen and a wonderful camaraderie. Every weekend Mandy prepared and supervised a two course meal then we all retired to the bar to get either, inebriated if the weather the following day was to be poor, or a few drinks and early night if flying was likely. We had many themed evenings and Christmas was well attended with pilots from others areas visiting. They were good days.

There were levels of achievement to aspire to and the first, after initially qualifying, was to obtain your Bronze certificate. On gaining this you could venture away from your flying site and ultimately gain cross country experience. The Bronze was awarded after completing a written test and of course flying tests which included practice landing out using a power glider. Your instructor would cut the engine and ask you to land thus you had to pick a safe landing site and set up to land safely and, at the optimum moment, the instructor would fire the engine and power away from the ground. He would thus have ascertained whether you would have landed safely. The written paper consisted of several parts including Air Law, Principals of Flight, Meteorology and Navigation.

I did the paper first under Mike Bond's tutelage and a few weeks later I did the flying test under the CFI (Chief Flying Instructor) Dave Stewart's tutelage. I did the flying test quite early in the day and was too uptight to ask the outcome and stewed all day not knowing. Dave knew this and let me stew. I found out by the fact that, when the control wagon was towed back to the hanger, there was a message scrawled on the blackboard on its side saying 'Gillian is buying the drinks in the bar tonight' Yowser!!!! Thank you Dave.

One flight I recall was not far from the airfield however I had got rather low over Ripon and cross wind, and suddenly realised I was in danger of not being able to make it back to the airfield. So I trekked at what I thought was best glide angle back to the airfield trying to aim as far down the landing area as possible. To say I was worried is to put it mildly, the correct term for how I felt is not printable. I do remember saying out loud 'mother help me' and she did. I came in very low over the A1, heaven only knows what the drivers on the road thought, and landed having completed no circuit as I did not have the height. And, after all that, all I was worried about was getting grounded. I was not grounded because I had done the safe thing. Lucky or what?

The next certificate to aspire to was the 'Silver' To obtain this you had to complete several requirements one of which was a 50 kilometre cross country landing at another site. One day I was all set to attempt the 50K. My little K6, a wood and fabric glider, which wasn't mine but I called it mine, was a little darling. It belonged to Hambleton's and another pilot took it up before me and kept it up a long time. By the time he came down the lift was waning but I still took off though the odds were stacked against me. I was tasked with taking a TP (turning point) photograph at Lumley reservoir and then hightailing south east to Pocklington. I got the TP photograph but the lift was dying and I could not make it to the next thermal, I was sinking so I had to land. I picked a clear field near Ripon, set up circuit and dutifully landed feeling dismal because the 50K was not to be and tense because I was landing out for the first time. Dishforth knew exactly where I was because I looked up and saw one of the power planes circling above – Dave Stewart had been watching me. I went to the farmer's house to phone Dishforth to ask for my 'crew'. Whenever attempting a cross country you had to set up your 'crew' beforehand, that is persuade other pilots to come and rescue you and the glider if you land out. I put my parachute on the wing knowing the glider was safe and went to wait at the roadside for my crew. Mike Bond and Neil Claughton and his girl came to rescue me and K6 and the farmer's wife and son also came out to the field. I took photographs and sent a letter of thanks with a photo to the little boy; I hope he remembers the day a lady landed in his Dad's field.

Flying in England, Scotland and Wales

A memorable flight I had was in September and I was flying in wave. You can reach great heights in wave achieving over 30,000 feet. I was only at about eight thousand feet and the sun was shining on the cloud bank and on my glider. It cast a shadow of the glider on the cloud bank, which looked like the white cliffs of Dover, and there was a complete rainbow all the way round the shadow. I did not have my camera with me. Durhh.

I went on to learn to drive the winch of all things. I think perhaps I was the only female at Dishforth doing this. It carried quite a bit of responsibility in that a huge amount of power was released on the strop to launch a glider and this speed had to be regulated. If a launch was too slow the pilot of the glider being launched would keep the glider nose down, if the speed was too fast, and thus potentially stressing the glider, then the pilot would wave off by moving the tail from side to side. If the speed did not slacken then the pilot would release the strop and land rather than stress the glider. If the speed is actually too slow there comes a point of no return in that air speed is fundamental to control, getting too high with a slow launch is very unsafe. Driving the winch really was a man's job in so far as if the strop broke it required some strength to work the ratchet tools to repair it as it consisted of many bands of steel wire. I did once release the strop whilst being winch launched as the speed was too slow which was slightly unnerving.

I stayed many times at Dishforth over the coming years as there was a women's bunkhouse and some pilots had caravans on site so I could use one of those when offered. When Tony and I took the pub I could not attend as often and joined Yorkshire Gliding Club at Sutton Bank in order to get some weekday flying in. I did not get to fly much up there but what I did up there was wonderful, it is a magnificent site to fly from.

These are pictures taken in Port Moak in Scotland

I was lucky enough to fly in the Black Mountains in Wales (above) and also in Scotland at Port Moak.

The Black Mountains were awesome, to use an American colloquialism. I went with Tony and Richard to Wales and we stayed with the Derek the farmer pilot who owned the site. On the day we were leaving he insisted I had to fly one last time before going. It was one the best flights I have ever experienced. The lift was working.

The Black Mountains are quite high, as was this site. The lift was 'wave' lift which is more prevalent in autumn. Long cigar shaped clouds are formed and on the lead side of these clouds phenomenal lift can occur. On this day the lift was unbelievable. We were in the lift virtually from take-off which I had never experienced before. I was flying with Derek and he told me the lift was at least 19 knots. The vario, in the glider we were in, would only register to 10 knot lift however he was experienced in high lift. To corroborate what he said I heard on the radio from another glider that the lift was registering 19 knots! The other airborne pilot later wrote an article in Sailplane and Gliding magazine and said that the lift topped at 21 knots that day. Imagine going up in one of those New York outside-building lifts at high speed with a lot of buffeting and some loud wind noise – that's the nearest picture I can paint. Brilliant. I even got to fly with John Bally – a champion pilot.

Port Moak in Scotland was a lovely flat site near Loch Leven with some great people running it. After a check flight I was clear to fly solo and on one of the days I was about the third/fourth into the air. It was a slightly hazy flat day but after scratching about I felt a little flutter and gently moved into it. *'Yahoo. Nah na na nah na. I've found the lift'* I shouted. I was very childish. When I got established in the thermal I got my camera out, I wasn't making that mistake again, and took a picture of other pilots on the ground scrambling to get their gliders on line for launching to catch the lift.

At Dishforth I took over as Site Treasurer of Hambleton's from Polly for a while and when Hambleton's left to go to another site I was lucky enough to be invited to stay with Cleveland's. I became bar manager as a job to qualify my membership. Eventually I had to give up flying due to personal circumstances and subsequent lack of funding, but I will never forget Dishforth.

I loved those years of flying and not least because of the people. Thank you all for making me air aware.

I particularly remember one day at Dishforth it was reported that a Lancaster was due to fly over. I flew that day but I did not see the Lancaster though I like to believe that I shared some of the same air space.

My time there helped me to have a greater understanding of the flying Dad did in the war.

I have to thank Eric Stephenson for clearing me for my very first solo flight, Dave Stewart for a lovely flight to Barnard Castle in July '86 and for my Bronze 'C' and Mike Bond for my Bronze 'C', Tony Simm for aerobatics, Alan Swales for the opportunity to fly power to Duxford Air Show, Terry Wilson for two long flights we did and he covered when I was funding challenged, Ben Benoist, Polly and Paul Whitehead, Foxy, Dave Campbell, Mandy, Colin, Wally and Fred, Jack, Pat Rowell, Jill Povall, Neil Claughton, Steve Ollender, Henry Pantin, Peter Wilson, Wendy and Martin all of you just for being. These are the people I had most contact with but there were very many others – if I have missed your name I apologise, some of my brain cells are leaking out in my fast approaching dotage.

..... And Then There Was Charles

Major Charles Edward Laidlaw (ret.) of the American Air Force to be precise. If America wanted a role model to epitomise a fine incontrovertibly upstanding 'All American' citizen then they should look no further than Charles E Laidlaw. I am proud to have him as my brother in law.

On Charles last tour of duty in England he was stationed at Menwith Hill and he, Paula, Jenny and James were able to live close to Dad in Pateley Bridge from July 1999 to June 2002. Every February Charles' squadron would go to Sheffield for a wreath laying ceremony at a monument to the US Air Crew of the Mi Amigo which had been lost on return from a bombing mission over Germany. Charles said *"it was a sad story really. The plane was damaged over Germany and only barely made it back to England. It was trying to crash land in a city park in Sheffield but the field was full of young lads playing football. The crew tried to wave the kids off the pitch, but the kids thought they were just waving so they waved back! At that point the skipper had two choices – either land on the field and take out those kids or divert from the field and take their chances. He opted for the latter and they crashed into a hill killing all on board. So in honour of selflessly saving those kids the City of Sheffield has a wreath laying ceremony to commemorate that date and invites nearby US forces to participate. One year I took Len along. He wore his usual blazer with medals and marched with us to the site and participated on the side-lines in the formalities. Then he came back to the Polish War Vets club for afters. I didn't realise that, after the fall of Poland, those Poles that had made it out settled in England and joined up in the British forces. They have a presence big enough in Sheffield to warrant their own Legion Club."*

So there they were eating *'typical British finger food – sausage rolls and cucumber sandwiches'* as Charles puts it. Us Brits (aka British people) really must up our game in the culinary quarter. Two very nice ladies came and sat next to them and it transpired that they were both WWII Veterans too. *"I think one was a nurse and the other was part of the RAF in air traffic control launching and recovering RAF bombers and directing RAF fighters whenever Gerry flew bombing missions over England. Well I think I got a glimmer of what Len was like 'back in the day' and probably between missions smoozing the lady folk. He was quite smooth with them and they got quite giddy in the presence of a real honest to God bomber flyboy. I had to do everything from laughing. It was all innocent enough, but I could see the sparkle in Len's eye while charming the ladies. It was cool!"*

While Charles and clan were still based in England Dad got Charles an honorary membership to the White Rose branch of the RAF Aircrew Association which is now sadly in its decline owing to dwindling numbers. It was however, and still is, a great source of information and comfort to the membership. Charles used to accompany Dad to the monthly luncheons which were held at Harrogate Cricket grounds. *"there were Spit pilots, Lanc. pilots and other aircraft pilots. In fact I recall talking to one guy who got to fly one of the RAF's first jet aircraft right at the end of the war. And I also got to speak to a couple of chaps who flew Spits in the Battle of Britain. I only wish I'd had enough sense to write down each and every one of those conversations and do some follow up research on their episodes in the war. But for me it was just a real honour to be allowed to associate with such an amazing group of guys; and I'll be forever grateful to Len for being such a good friend and allowing me to be a part of his amazing life!"*

Over the years Charles and family spent tours of duty intermittently in England and, after their final relocation from England to Boston, Charles became involved in the running of an Anglo/American upgrade project at RAF Fylingdales in North Yorkshire. He made many trips across the Atlantic to coordinate the American part of the project and we all saw much of him, Dad in particular.

Charles recounts *"during my many chats with my RAF counterpart at Fylingdales, Wing Commander Paul Maguire, I mentioned that my father-*

in-law was in the RAF and flew Lancs during WWII. He instantly became intrigued and on learning that Len actually lived in the area he insisted that I bring him back to the base for a visit. Paul set up a tour of the actual radar facility for Len and he arranged a luncheon at the Officer's Mess in his honour. One of Paul's reasons for wanting to do this was that he relished the opportunity to host 'Spanner' and welcoming him back to the RAF for a visit.

During my many trips associated with the Fylingdales upgrade I would sometimes bring colleagues of mine over to meet Len. I brought First Lieutenant Jason Anis, one of my young action officers, on one occasion. Len took great pride in hosting visits from American military and was always the source of amazing 'war stories'. Every one of my colleagues who met him was blown away at what he accomplished during the war. That is of course when they could understand him! Most folks had a real hard time with his Yorkshire accent! But for all of that they found him intriguing and a joy. Others that I recall introducing him to were our lead logistician, retired USAF Colonel Mike Fitz, my former commander and best boss I ever had – USAF Colonel Mike Cox, and good friend and all-round-good- guy Ken Cole – head of our Site Activation Team and contractors. I know there were others, but they say your memory is the third thing to go – and I can't remember the other two...."

Charles likes his jokes.

Whenever he came to England Charles flew into Leeds/Bradford airport, rented a car and then set off to Pateley Bridge to stop off en route to RAF Fylingdales. He usually made it to Pateley just in time to meet Len at the Crown Hotel for his midday sandwiches which were kindly provided daily FOC by another of my brother-in-laws and landlord of the Crown – Dennis Audsley. Dennis too was ex RAF and a retired Air Traffic Sergeant. Charles said "I have spent many a day in there with Len chewing the cud so to speak, and talking 'air force'"

He would then go over to Fylingdales, work the week and then come over to Leeds on the Friday to see 'us kids' as he called us! I, of course, am a lot more ancient than he is! We would do the usual – a good old chin wag, an Indian curry and for the boys – beer, for me – wine, but sometimes in moments of depravity we resorted to Gentleman Jack (a more refined variant of Jack Daniel's whiskey). At this point I usually left them to it to do the 'good Ol' Boys' chin wag putting the world to rights and achieving nothing more than total inebriation and a whole lot of fun! Warren and Charles are good buddies. On Saturday we would 'goof around' as Charles put it (such strange colloquialisms have these Americans) then on Sunday he would set off to Pateley again to take Dad and Nancy out for dinner before getting back to Fylingdales. They usually went to the Chequers up near Markington not far from where Dad was born. Charles said it was a lot of fun, actually as he says 'we had a blast', and he remembered those meals to be warm and fun.

Wing Commander Paul Maguire (RAF) Warrant Officer
Leonard N. Watson (Spanner – RAF retired) Major Charles Laidlaw
(American Airforce) at Fylingdales

Nidderdale Show and Fair

Otherwise known as Pateley Show and Pateley feast to the natives, this is excitement in its utmost element. This annual event is usually on the third Monday in September with the feast arriving the Friday before to ensure a whole weekend of frivolities.

In the fifties a small contingent would travel to Dacre village feast field after the Pateley show but this no longer happens as the land has been built up.

The local children had a field day at the feast and most got to go each day if only to stand around and watch the action. Oh how I remember those early teenage days eyeing up a new boy in town on the big roundabout. It was quite fascinating to see the 'feast lads' – those who took your money – jumping on and off the rides whilst they were travelling at breakneck speeds. The big roundabout drew all the teenagers as it was accompanied by loud music. In the early years mud was an accepted facility of the feast and I well remember falling flat on my face in a white dress to be clarted up to the nines and most disgruntled. Now I look back on that fondly. Today the feast site area has a tarmac base so the fun of mud is obsolete.

Naturally it was customary to have a go on the shooting and, almost without fail, win a dodgy piece of pottery or, in later years a plastic toy or key ring. Mum certainly collected a very random selection of crockery that we proudly presented her with each September.

The show is a very strongly attended event in the Dales today. Pateley Bridge, and in particular the High Street, is always awash with people. All the pubs do a roaring trade and it is usually standing room only in them. It is customary for many locals to 'do the rounds' going from one pub to the other but also, of course, to go into the show.

The show started in the 1920's and now attracts around 14,000 people on a good day. The weather can have a slightly adverse effect but only slight as the mud seems to add to the ambience. Sloshing around from show tent to show tent is great fun but when the sun shines it is even more fun.

Many celebrities have graced the show with their presence, some for reporting purposes, some producing an individual programme and some judging. In 2009 I observed Janet Street-Porter, who has a property in the Dale, being filmed talking to one of the exhibitor ladies in the Women's Institute tent.

Tents include the Women's Institute/Craft tent which offers many displays of locally made cakes, preserves and handiwork; the Flower tent which has a huge amount of beautiful displays; a children's tent with local children's crafts; plus rabbits, guinea pigs, chickens, cockerels, and many I cannot recall. Then of course there are the tents with the main reason for the show – the farm animals – cattle, sheep, pigs and dogs all are paraded for judging. I have, more than once, seen a calf being born at the show. There would occasionally be the runaway bull intent on dragging its handler away but these always ended happily.

As children we would hang about in the last hours of the show and we could buy, or even have given, some of the flowers from the displays which we diligently took home to Mum. She was often presented with beautiful flowers with huge heads too big for our mediocre vases.

The main arena hosts the show jumping and dressage events, vehicle displays and motorcycle stunts. On the periphery of the grounds sheep dog trails are also held. And to accompany all of this entertainment at its best, there is a Brass Band and of course the obligatory beer tents.

There are very many trade stands now which were not so evident in early years. Agricultural vehicles are displayed – many from eons ago along with cars and vans.

This is where Spanner enters the picture. Many years ago he got the chance to buy an old 1948 Morris 8 series car. This was in a state of disrepair but it gave Dad something to occupy himself with and to have an on-going project in his 'wind down' years. Winding down did not come easy to him and, given half a chance, he would have kept on working even when his physical capabilities were becoming a hindrance. Like most very active people he found it hard to accept a decline in capability.

So enter stage left his little Morris car. He loved his car and he refurbished it, repaired and tended it, polished and nurtured it and the result was a very attractive classic old car of 1948 origin and in better shape than me – of the same age!

He took great pride in taking the car to shows and naturally Nidderdale Show was on his agenda.

He would sit on a chair by his car, or inside if it was raining, and talk to anyone interested in his pride and joy. Many of his contemporaries would specifically visit him and he looked forward each year to seeing them. Naturally any family members would detour to ensure he was included in the show safari.

Two old warriors and a 1948 model
Spanner and Joe Hardcastle

In recent years my husband, Warren, was walking through one of the ginnels in the High Street and found a little shop selling postcards. What should be displayed in all its glory but little Morris. It was a picture taken of the car driving down the High Street with Dad at the wheel. The copyrighters/printers were kind enough to let him have a blown up print of the original which he proudly displayed on his wall.

As the years pass even those who have left the dale still wander back intermittently to attend the show. It holds so many happy memories for a big load of dales folk.

Wing Commander Ernest Millington DFC

O ne Sunday evening in November some years ago Terry had the television on but he wasn't paying much attention to it. He did however notice that someone was interviewing a Wing Commander Millington who was a labour MP for Chelmsford after World War II. The mention of the Second World War sparked his interest and he started to listen. The programme was 'Anglia at Peace.' *"I came up to Pateley at Christmas and mentioned it to Dad and he said 'that was the chap I flew with in the war"*

After Christmas one of those odd recession periods that intermittently rear their heads leaving the construction industry the first to suffer meant Terry was having a lean spell. So in January at another loose end he started thumbing through the yellow pages and found a television number which he rang. They in turn put him in touch with a company in Norwich that had made the programme in which WC Millington had appeared. *"I drafted a letter to Mr. Millington, with another letter and stamps for forwarding, and sent it off to the production company. A few weeks later I got a phone call from Dad. He said 'do you know who 'as just rung me after fifty four years? Mi old Wing Commander Millington' 'I said that's good Dad. Then half an 'our later I got a call from Wing Commander Millington himself thanking me for getting them back together again"*

It was sheer luck that Terry had some time on his hands and was able to pursue it. Dad was over the moon to be in contact with his Skipper again.

Dad and his Skipper then continued to write to each other and exchanged Christmas cards over the following years. One Christmas a card did not come from him and Dad was concerned. Apparently Wing Commander Millington DFC had passed away 10th May 2009 at the age of ninety three. He was the last surviving member of the wartime House of Commons. In 2005/6 he published his autobiography entitled 'Was That Really Me'. He had said that he had been struck by the compliments paid to his command and the sense of loyalty that had grown between the airmen he knew.

Dad was upset to learn of his passing and asked me to write his condolences to his wife which I duly did. She very kindly responded which Dad was happy to receive. He still remembered his Skipper with utmost admiration.

Gill Now

In January 2008 I was diagnosed with throat cancer. I remember going to the hospital with Warren and knowing, before I was told, what the diagnosis was going to be. We were struck numb.

We came out of the hospital and it was just turning dusk and I could hear birds singing, I looked up and saw the tops of the tall trees swaying in the breeze. I told Warren that the birds were singing for me.

We went home in a state of unpreparedness, if there is such a word, of not knowing how to deal with or approach this new big chapter. It was hard to tell my family, it was hard to see the hurt they were feeling. Warren, Sally and Richard were obviously distraught and trying hard not to show it. Strangely this seemed to affect me more than the fact that I was possibly not long for this world.

I neither took readily to, nor endured without complications, the treatment. Everyone is different, in the side effects they may experience, in their recovery rate and in residual physical effects after treatment. I suffered a great deal of sickness and lost much weight. The treatment I underwent was a little chemotherapy and 35 sessions of radiotherapy. This is a highly invasive treatment but it is very effective.

Cancer does make you prone to some emotional outbursts but it also makes you appreciate and value even ordinarily little things so much more. There is a definite transformation and a new acceptance of what is, and more importantly what is not, important in life.

Warren was, oh I just cannot find an acceptable word in my thesaurus to give him the accolade he richly deserves. The best I can do is this little tribute I wrote:

True Colours

If I could paint in the colours you reflect
I would be very rich indeed,
But I have bathed in them and been cocooned in them
Whilst I have been so very ill
And nothing material or otherwise on this earth
Could make me any richer

I got wonderful support from my family over the coming months. Terry and Linda promptly came up from Cambridge and we tottered out of the hospital to a local bistro for coffee promising to come there again when I was well.

On hearing the news Paula jumped on a plane from Alabama and stayed with us for about six weeks and was brilliant support for my flagging vitality and stoicism. She was with me when my treatment started and she helped both Warren and I get through those rather stressful weeks. My daughter Sally, sister Marie, niece Mel, niece Tash and great niece Amy all ran in the Race for Life that is organised annually at the Great Yorkshire Show ground in Harrogate (Arrigut). They video'd it and brought their achievements into the ward and we all sat around giggling at their efforts. I have one of their medals hanging in my kitchen where it now lives. As do I. I am clear of cancer after my treatment and am now on annual checks. I do have some after effects that I will not go into, but I have been told to get on with the rest of my life now.

I have nothing but admiration for all the people at St. James Hospital Bexley Oncology Wing. I cannot praise them enough for their dedication and care. I felt I was in safe, efficient and knowledgeable hands from the onset. I also had magnificent aftercare from the wonderful district nurses, my Macmillan nurse and my GP practice. The National Health Service should be venerated and not denigrated as readily as it has been recently.

My cup is half full and I feel very lucky.

Air Trails

When I was a young child I was fascinated by those things in the air that left a trail of what looked to me like long clouds behind them. I was so engrossed I would stare at them as they slowly dissipated. I was told they were aeroplanes but pictures of them were not prolific at the time. You only saw a vapour trail occasionally but today when the sky is blue it rather looks like the angels have been playing tic-tac-toe. I did not know then that I would eventually fly planes. When Dad was younger I don't remember him talking about the war so we children were blissfully unaware of what he had been through in the war or that he had actually flown. If I had known I would have been totally awestruck. Only as Dad got older did he venture onto the subject. This 'venturing' eventually took on the form of very regular instruction on 'what went on in the war', and it *was* instruction and we were expected to listen. He had spent most of his adult life in charge of one thing or another and he was not for changing in his dotage. Initially it was immensely interesting but sadly as time progressed Dad became repetitive, but I was aware that sometimes a new little snippet of information emerged in his regular excursions into his past. I became engrossed in listening to all he had to say and even as he repeated himself I became more and more aware that it was of profound importance to know 'what went in in the war'.

It was during my convalescence period that I took to visiting Dad quite regularly and we chin wagged or rather I listened to his reminiscences. This is when the book idea first hatched and it became something for me to concentrate on and take my mind off health issues. Over the coming months, which developed into a couple of years through my inability to concentrate or give it regular attention, a story emerged. Spanner was about to go public.

When Warren and I drove from the hospital, after being given the devastating news of my diagnosis, I was engrossed in looking at the landscape with a new awareness. It was as if I had only just noticed the grass and trees but they were grey in the twilight. I remember thinking it was sad that when it was dark all those lovely green colours became grey. My little world then was grey.

Lincoln, after the bombs were dropped, was grey. All the cities after the bombs were dropped were grey. Even the skies from whence the bombs came were often grey. The mood on returning, of the proud and brave men who had flown over enemy territory and carried out their wartime role, was grey. They had to drop bombs to fight this war. It is inconceivable now for any of us to remotely want to consider being in that same position to fight fire with fire in order to bring on the end of a war. These days we try to avert war and encourage peace, but sometimes to no avail. This was a war that was killing hundreds daily and would continue so to do until one side or the other won.

Can we truly accept that losing the war was an alternative? To succumb to a regime that destroyed its own people would have been catastrophic for humanity.

We have striven to justify our part in dropping bombs and much has been written about this. Some have objected to and others have concurred with the decision that was initially made. But it is a sad fact that very few if any wars have been won by being placid and any resultant carnage from relinquishing all rights and 'giving up' may well have exceeded the actual death toll of the war. Who is to know? We can all surmise.

Bomber Command Memorial

Can current generations begin to understand the depth of feeling, the sheer despondency, the emboldening from battles won and the despair of those lost and the uncertainty that prevailed? Yet the stoical backbone of strength that epitomised the British people at this historic time shone through. Bomber Command played their part with valour.

..... And some 65 years later Bomber Command finally received the go ahead for an official public memorial in Green Park. Their heroic part in history that helped the British people to be who they are today is acknowledged. Our forefathers are our foundation and our salvation. These men and women did their duty on our behalf. How sad that it has taken so long.

It is a fact that out of 125,000 air crew 55,573 were killed, with another 8,403 wounded and 9,838 ending up in German POW camps. To put this in perspective it has been recorded that the RAF lost 700 men in just one night.

Sadly in May 2011 the last survivor of World War I passed away, the very last witness to this significant historical era.

The Bomber Command Association stated it was losing 40 to 50 members a month. Soon there will only be a very few left to recall this part of history.

It is to be hoped that this memorial, planned to be unveiled in spring 2012, is unveiled while there are still members of Bomber Command alive who can witness an acknowledgement of their contribution to our future.

FORM 1767
(REVISED OCT. 1943)

ROYAL AIR FORCE

FLYING LOG BOOK
FOR
NAVIGATORS
AIR BOMBERS
AIR GUNNERS
FLIGHT ENGINEERS

Name   L. H. Watson

Date	Hour	Aircraft Type and No.	Pilot	Duty
JULY .20		LANC III P	F/LT MILLINGTON	ENGINEER
22		LANC III P	F/LT MILLINGTON	.. ..
24		LANC III Q	F/LT MILLINGTON	.. ..
24		LANC III P	F/LT MILLINGTON	.. ..
25		LANC III P	F/LT MILLINGTON	.. ..
25		LANC. III P	F/LT MILLINGTON	.. ..
28		LANC III P	F/LT MILLINGTON	.. ..
28		LANC III P.	F/LT MILLINGTON	.. ..
30		LANC III P	F/LT MILLINGTON	.. ..
31		LANC III P	F/LT MILLINGTON	.. ..

240

	Time carried forward :—		
		49·15	26·40

REMARKS (including results of bombing, gunnery, exercises, etc.)	Flying Times	
	Day	Night
H2S CROSS COUNTRY + H.L.B	3·15	
FIGHTER AFFIL + NFT	1·25	
ACCEPTANCE TEST	1·35	
OPERATION. DONGES.		5·50
NFT	0·10	
OPERATION STUTTGART		8·50
NFT	1·10	
OPERATION STUTTGART		7·10
OPERATION CANNES		
OPERATION	4·55	
TOTAL TIME ...	55·30	46·30

241

Date	Hour	Aircraft Type and No.	Pilot	Duty
AUG 1.		LANC III P	F/LT MILLINGTON	ENGINEER
2		LANC III P	F/LT MILLINGTON	.. ..
3		LANC III P	F/LT MILLINGTON	.. ..
4		LANC III P	F/LT MILLINGTON	.. ..
5		LANC III P	F/LT MILLINGTON	.. ..
16		LANC III P LM648	F/LT MILLINGTON	.. ..
17		LANC III P LM648	S/L MILLINGTON	.. ..
22		LANC III P LM648	S/L MILLINGTON	.. ..
25		LANC III P LM648	S/L MILLINGTON	.. ..

242

REMARKS (including results of bombing, gunnery, exercises, etc.)	Flying Times	
Time carried forward :—	55.30	46.30
	Day	Night
OPERATION LA BRETEQUE	3.50	
OPERATION TROSSY ST MAXIMIN	4.05	
OPERATION TROSSY. ST MAXIMIN. HIT BY FLAK. HYDRAULICS U/S LANDED AT WITTERING.	4.10	
WITTERING TO BASE	0.25	
OPERATION ST LEODESSERONE TWO ENGINES ON FIRE LANDED WITH TWO ENGINES A BURST TYRE NO HYDRAULICS AND INTER COM U/S AT FORD	4.45	
OPERATION STETTIN		7.45
TO DUNHOLME	0.20	
NFT	0.35	
OPERATION DARMSTART		8.20
TOTAL TIME ...	73.40	62.35

243

There's a welcome in the Dale

See the tall roof on the right where Len got hooked up

The Memorial Hall today

Thruscross reservoir – can you hear the church bell?

Leonard Newby Watson
20.3.1922 – 14.6.2011
aka Spanner

British Legion marching down Pateley Bridge High Street

Royal British Legion

On the 6th April 2011 I went to Pateley to meet the two Brians. Mere youngsters in their early seventies both are staunch supporters of the Royal British Legion and have active rolls in the Nidderdale branch. Brian Weatherhead is very tall whereas Brian Hicks is somewhat shorter and it brought to mind *'Bless 'em all, Bless 'em all, the long and the short and the tall'* It was a great pleasure to meet them.

Brian Weatherhead is part of the Weatherhead dynasty well known in the dale for their butchers business and shop at the bottom of Pateley High Street.

Harry Weatherhead started the business back in 1876 little knowing that it would still be going today with their fifth generation at the helm. Brothers Brian and Ian with Ian's son Andrew are the current stalwarts.

He was in the forces from 1959 to 1961 and was initially based at Catterick Garrison in the Royal Signals. He later went to Woking in Surrey for sixteen weeks training and then into the Royal Military Police and sent out to Verden in Germany. He has been a member of the British Legion for 10 years and is Nidderdale branch Treasurer and Vice Chairman on the Memorial Hall Committee for the British Legion.

Brian Hicks moved to the dales in the 90's. He was in the Royal Lincolnshire Regiment as a National Serviceman 1954-56 and ended up in the intelligence section. He served in Germany and was later posted to Malaya to 63 Ghurkha brigade HQ for about 6 months. The Ghurkha's were fighting communist terrorists in the jungle. When he left the forces he enlisted with the Territorial Army in the Parachute Regiment. He left the TA due to family priorities. He is now branch Secretary.

He was keen to talk of his childhood growing up in Lincolnshire where he saw much of the RAF activity often seeing the aircraft overhead leaving and coming home. His mother worked at the Hotel Central and used to come home with stories that she had heard from the RAF lads that drank there on their days off. He specifically remembers she told him how they used to amuse themselves. One of them would invariable end up standing on a table and issuing forth with a chant to which the other lads would respond raucously. This led to very loud jollities set in for the evening. His mother said they enjoyed themselves like there was no tomorrow which was probably how they viewed it. She once had a photograph sent to her from one of the RAF crews showing a line-up of men in front of a Lancaster, it was signed -

'To Fran, you pull 'em up and we sup 'em up'

Membership of the RBL has sadly been declining over the years in the dale. Originally there were several branches in the dale – Summerbridge and Dacre, Birstwith and Lower Nidderdale and Pateley Bridge. Pateley branch finished in the 80's and the remaining members joined with Summerbridge and eventually the name got changed to Nidderdale branch in January 1989 and they meet every two months.

The Armistice parade in Pateley is always carried out on November 11th on whatever day it falls. The Legion branch organises the parade, which used to progress down the High street. It now forms in the showground, and, with local civic dignitaries they march to the War Memorial.

This service is always well attended by people paying homage to those in the dale who gave their lives and also to remember with gratitude those who still serve in the nations conflicts for our freedom.

When Spanner joined them he proudly marched in their ranks and more recently up until 2009 he led the Branch dignitaries taking the salute.

The following picture is of men ready to march down the High Street in a parade to the park – Len 'Spanner' Watson, Ron Hodgson, Brian Weatherhead, Fred Spence, Peter Chadwick, Joe Hardcastle, Chris Sexton (Branch Standard Bearer) and John Simpson (Branch President)

Ready to march

The values of the Royal British Legion are Remembrance, Hope, Comradeship, Selflessness and Service. They offer help to all serving and ex-service people and their families including all those still fighting today. They also have care homes and break centres across England, Wales and Ireland.

The very first Legion Poppy Day was held 11th November 1921 and Remembrance Day is a key annual event in the British calendar. 2011 marks the 90th Anniversary of The Royal British Legion.

Lest we forget.

We shall not.

Spanner has held court and proudly told of his service days to many in the dale and it has been a joy and a privilege to have had the opportunity to write this.

I have learned much. Thanks Dad.

Glad you came back.

Lister House

Spanner, now unfortunately on the home stretch, suffered a couple of strokes followed by a fall in February 2010 and he became hospitalised. He maintained a proclivity towards holding forth about his war exploits and, each time he did he often managed to remember a little more, until his mental agility started to wane.

He spent many weeks in Harrogate District Hospital before being transferred to Ripon Hospital where he stayed for a couple of months. He was wheelchair bound by this time and it was obvious to everyone but Dad that he would not be able to go home.

In July 2010 he was taken to Lister House British Legion Residential Home. The home is a lovely building with a tank outside, and a large propeller, from which aircraft it derives I have not ascertained. The care and facilities are excellent and though we took some of his pictures in to make him feel more at home he still maintained he would go home eventually.

He was a bit gung ho with his wheelchair though and led the nurses a merry dance. He would go as fast as possible with little regard for any consequences and bombing into things became a fun thing for him. He was told off by the nurses so he *'capped 'em'* as he told it. He would slow down as he went passed the nurses' station and speed up immediately after. Consequentially we had to have his wheelchair governed without his knowledge!

What has been particularly good about him being in Lister House is that many friends and family were able to visit him. His close friend Nancy being there very regularly and many of his former employees often popping in.

He still maintained his membership of The Aircrew Association, though it no longer accepts membership purely because membership is very naturally dwindling. He also maintained his membership of The British Legion, of which he has been very proud to be a part of since he joined in 1999.

His friend Joe Hardcastle also came into Lister House at the beginning of 2011. Dad was 89 years young on March 20th 2011 and Joe 93 years young. They both took part in the marches down the High Street in Pateley Bridge on Remembrance Day.

I often took book chapters in to Dad and read them to him which helped keep his spirits up. He has had a lot of pleasure in the acknowledgements he has had over the years for his part in the war.

Spanner outside Lister House November 2010

Epilogue

In the early hours of 14th June 2011 the telephone rang and we got the saddest news.

Dad was gone.

Spanner passed away quietly in his sleep at Lister House. His page in history was sadly now completed.

On my last but one visit to see him I stood up and saluted him. Typically, even though he was extremely poorly, he told me off because I had got it wrong.

"Ah" I said "long way up, short way down"

He nodded.

I did it again.

He smiled.

This is a brief excerpt from his Obituary in the Nidderdale Herald:

Tribute to Local Legend

'His funeral on 23rd June at St Cuthbert's Church was choreographed beautifully by The Reverend Peter Dunbar. Lofthouse and Middlesmoor Brass Band provided much of the music along with the organist. A poem and reading were given by local people and a tribute was read by his daughter. A strong representation of the British Legion attended along with Standard Bearers. Just before the cortege set off from Kingsclere the heavens opened up; this was doubtless a sign from Len that he was disgruntled he was not able to share the day but, had he been able to, he would have been proud.

The following day his ashes were laid to rest at St. Mary's, attended by his family and the vicar and the RAF very kindly, but totally unaware, provided a fly past of two planes.

Perhaps Len aka Spanner was still pulling strings.

'God Bless'

Lots of Thank you's

Thank you to

... all the staff at Harrogate District Hospital that looked after Len when he first went into hospital in February 2010,

... the staff, especially the nurses at Ripon hospital who nursed him and waved at him every time they passed his bed,

... Marie for running around for him, his wish was her command,

... and a special thanks to the staff, carers and nurses at Lister House who have the task of nursing, caring and tending to the residents in their dotage years and which they do with a kindly smile and a bit of banter,

... Binns Hearing Healthcare of Apperley Bridge for keeping him in the land of the hearing

... for Len's care

Thank you to

... My husband Warren for his absolute care,

... Special thanks to the wonderful team at St. James's Hospital Bexley Wing Oncology, for their expertise and for care and for managing to make me feel I mattered and was not just another NHS statistic,

... all the technical staff and the nursing staff who also took care of me,

... my GP practice from whom I would never change,

... the district nurses – Margaret and her team who attended me regularly and were wonderful and very supportive, and Macmillan nurse Joanne,

... Fresenius for efficiency and reliability at its best,

... for Gill's care

And Even More Thank You's

S panner (aka 'our Len' aka 'Leonard' aka 'Len') and Gill would like to thank -

All Spanners' family – daughters and son, their husbands, wives, children and children's children for playing a huge part in his life

Betty – Spanner's wife – gone but never forgotten

Nancy – Spanner's close friend and confidant over the past couple of decades

Wing Commander Millington for being Spanner's skipper and hero

The rest of the magnificent crew of the Lancaster – Scotty, Jimmy, Basil, Blondie and Ginger

Terry and Marie for delving into their past and pulling out long forgotten stuff – it was an eye opener guys

Joe Hardcastle – for his friendship and sharing his memories and contributing his wonderful account of war on the ground

June Watson for sharing her memories, for being a lovely friend with her husband Jim and contributing her delightful poem

Major Charles Laidlaw (rtd. American Air force) for his support and sharing his memories

Frank Dean for sharing his memories and contributing his own delectable Dales insight writings

Terry Thorpe for sharing his memories

Peter Chadwick for sharing his memories

Ian Eglin (Eggy) for sharing his memories

Paul Ripley for sharing his memories

All the men who worked for Len for the better part of 50 years

John and Barbara Breckon for Dalestar memories and musical input

Gladys Blakeson for Lofthouse and Middlesmoor Brass Band memories

Mary Metcalfe for some dales background

John Richmond – for friendship and contribution of a good ear and supplying publications of great interest

Dennis Audsley – mine host at The Crown Hotel in Pateley, for free lunch and coffee for Len for many years

The lovely people of Pateley Bridge and Nidderdale

My husband Warren who produced posters, leaflets and business cards and an excellent website and who nursed me without complaint and without whom this book would never have been completed

All my readers – Sally Kendrew, Marie Cluderay, Linda Watson, Anthony Henson, Martyn Fryer and Dave Ormandy for their critique

… and special thanks to Marie for being my Pateley PA and Dad's general DB

The Air Crew Association for continued support

Brian Weatherhead and Brian Hicks for British Legion memories and information

The British Legion for putting honour and caring first in an acknowledgement of those who fought in the wars

Mr Stan Beer for playing the most beautiful Last Post at Spanners funeral

and last but not least – The Lancaster Bomber

Contents